THE
ALCHEMY
OF
SUCCESS

THE ALCHEMY OF SUCCESS

Anthony Mora

Dunhill Publishing Co.
New York

The Alchemy Of Success

A DUNHILL HARDCOVER EDITION

Published by:
Dunhill Publishing Company
a division of the Zinn Publishing Group

Copyright © 1997 by Anthony Mora

ISBN: 0-935016-21-X

Printed in the United States of America

Library of Congress Cataloging-in-Publication Data

Mora, Anthony.
    The alchemy of success / Anthony Mora.
       p. cm.
    ISBN: 0-935016-21-X (pbk : alk. cloth)
    1. Advertising. 2. Mass media. 3. Public
    Relations. I. Title
HF5823.M57   1997
659--dc21   97-11690
                                CIP

Dedicated To Dad

Alchemist of the Heart

ACKNOWLEDGMENT

With thanks to David Zinn, the world's most original
and creative publisher.

Steve Allen, Kevin Thanrow, Susan Kaplan
and Thomas Brennan, the backbone of
Anthony Mora Communications, Inc.

And to Ann, my wife,
confidant and ever-growing beacon.

TABLE OF CONTENTS

Acknowledgment
Introduction

INTRODUCTION

The media explosion is echoing around the world. There are media outlets for all tastes and ages, spanning the gamut from *Larry King* and *Howard Stern* to *C-Span* and *MTV's News.* Along with 18 regional cable channels that offer 'round-the-clock local news, there are *CNN, MS-NBC,* the *Fox News Channel,* and *CNBC.* Local news stations now offer six or seven hours of daily news. The 40-billion-plus U.S. newspaper industry boasts well over 1500 daily papers, and talk radio has exploded both regionally and nationally. As of 1994, there were a total of 11,556 radio stations in the U.S. and there are over 550 million radios in the country, which averages out to about two radios per person. The Net, a still young, grand experiment, is ever growing and revolutionizing the way we communicate. That is a lot of media.

Never before have people been able to share information on such a global scale and with such speed. Along with newspapers, magazines, radio, TV, and the Internet, more and more avenues of communication are becoming available. It is possible to do an interview in the morning and have a story saturate the nation by lunchtime.

Media exposure can legitimize and validate a business, sell products, bring in clients, forge new alliances, bring you in contact with benefactors you never knew existed, and take you into the offices, boardrooms, and even bedrooms of the most powerful people in the world. Media exposure can help build businesses with dizzying speed.

The Most Powerful MarketingTool

Why is media exposure such a powerful tool? Simple. What makes or breaks most businesses? Referrals, or the lack thereof—word of mouth. For example, if the owner of a restaurant sings the praises of his cuisine, you may listen but, unless you're awfully naïve, you'd be at least somewhat cynical. It's his business to praise his business. But, if you come across a patron of that restaurant, who has no vested interest in the business, and that person sings the praises of the service, the wine, and the Chicken Alfredo, chances are, you'll not only believe that person, you'll probably be eating there within the month. Business growth basically comes down to a very low-tech, old-as-the-hills process: word-of-mouth.

So, what if there was a way of magnifying the word-of-mouth effect? What if you could nationally broadcast refered your city, state, country, or around the world? That's not only power, that's akin to magic. And that's what the *Alchemy of Success* is all about—harnessing the media's power, and focusing the magic of the media on you and your business.

Unlike any other form of marketing, effective media placement can help establish you as an expert in your field and showcase you, your business, talent, or product locally, nationally, and internationally. Through media placement, you are the story, you are news.

Leaping Into The Deep

Effective media placement is a remarkably powerful, effective and exciting process, but it has become a sophisticated process, which requires preparation, knowledge, and an overall game plan. Leaping into the deep before you know how to swim often results in drowning. It's important to learn the process, study the media, and learn the hows and whys of media placement.

The tools in this book work. You can use the magic of the media to create success in your business and in your life, but first set the groundwork, give some thought to what you're setting in motion. *The Alchemy of Success* is a skill that must be learned. Remember the tale of the *Sorcerer's Apprentice?* He activated the magic before he had mastered the craft and learned his mistake the hard way. It takes time, patience, and dedication, but once you have mastered the art and learned the *Alchemy of Success,* you can transform your dreams to reality.

Let the magic begin.

Chapter One

Understanding The Magic

1

Understanding The Magic

The Alchemy of Success concentrates exclusively on one aspect of public relations: effective media placement, also known as publicity (placing stories in magazines and newspapers, as well as radio, TV, and the Internet). The term "public relations" can entail a number of services, including market research, crisis management and communications, direct mail and mailing lists, special event management, database marketing, public relations counsel, issues and crisis management, community relations, internal communications, advertising, research, Internet marketing and publishing, and publicity and media placement.

Media Placement

My company does one thing and one thing only: media placement. We place our clients in newspapers and magazines, as well as on TV, the radio, and the Internet. We have placed clients in all forms of media, from small community newspapers, business newsletters, and cable access programs to such major outlets as *Time*, *People*, *The Wall Street Journal*, and *Today*. I've had clients who have continued to receive calls from media that was placed over a year ago, and others whose businesses were established by one well-placed article or TV appearance. Effective media placement truly is magic. I have

3

seen the magic of media change the lives of small business owners, physicians, corporate executives, attorneys, entertainers, artists, and business people from all walks of life. Used effectively and creatively, media placement is a fascinating and powerful tool.

How Do I Know If I Need Publicity?

· Could you benefit by reaching a greater share of your target audience?
· Do you want to introduce your business or skill to a broader-based market or audience?
· Would it help for you to be perceived as a leader in your field?
· Would it help your career to gain local and national exposure in TV, radio, and print?
· Do you want your business to grow, your product to sell, or your skill or talent to be viewed by hundreds, thousands, or possibly millions?

If you answered yes to any of the above, ask no further—you need public relations.

The truth is that almost everyone can benefit from public relations. Think of it. All of us have discovered a new product, business, or service from a magazine article or TV segment. Now it's time to turn that equation around, let others discover who you are by picking up a magazine or turning on the news. Nearly all businesses can profit from an effective publicity or media campaign. If you answered yes to any of the above questions, you need it.

Should I Handle My Own Publicity?

Should you handle your own publicity or media placement? No. Can you? Definitely.

Effective media placement is a full-time job. It takes skill, know-how, persistence, and contacts. The purpose of this book is to teach you the art of the *Alchemy of Success*. Media placement entails more than writing releases and putting together press kits. If you do it haphazardly or incorrectly, you're better off not doing it at all. The last thing you want to do is alienate the press, which is usually what happens when a well-meaning but inexperienced person tries his or her hand at media placement.

Media placement is a skill that needs to be learned and understood. None of us would decide to give open-heart surgery a try, or decide suddenly to overhaul a car transmission—well, at least most of us wouldn't—but hundreds of people decide that they can handle their own publicity without any prior knowledge or training whatsoever. An effective publicity campaign is well strategized and thought out. It is a cumulative process that builds day by day and month by month.

Your Options

If you are thinking of launching a media campaign for your business or career, you basically have four options: hire a public relations firm, hire someone in-house to do your public relations for you, hire a public relations consultant, or put together your own public relations campaign. The following chapters will teach you the tools and give you the information you need to implement an effective and successful media campaign yourself, as well as how to hire a public relations firm, PR consultant, or in-house publicist. But, whether you have decided to do your own public relations and want to learn the hows and whys of putting together a successful campaign, or, you are hiring a company to do it for you and want to learn the right questions to ask in order to hire the right firm, the information in this book is essential.

So You Think You Know PR?

I can't emphasize enough what a powerful medium this is. I have seen both businesses and careers launched through media placement, but I have also witnessed campaigns that went nowhere. The latter is usually due to ignorance of the process.

I've been lucky in that I've had the opportunity to see how publicity works from both sides of the street. My background is that of a journalist and magazine editor, which has given me a unique opportunity to see how publicists and media placement worked. I would daily be barraged by press releases, press kits, and phone calls from publicists and others trying to convince me to run a story on themselves or their clients. The trouble was that few of them gave me stories to run with; nine times out of ten, all they were offering was hype—smoke and mirrors. Some were so pushy or abrasive that not only did I not run their stories, I eventually refused to take their calls. They became a nuisance, people to be avoided. It is easy to alienate the press, which is why it is so important to adhere to each of the steps outlined in this book and learn the process. Don't assume you know what you're doing; I can all but guarantee you that you don't. And why should you? This isn't your business. You were never taught the fine points of publicity. So take your time. Read the entire book before you attempt to launch a campaign yourself. Once you set the magic in motion, it takes on a life of its own. Without setting it on the proper course, you can end up with more problems than solutions. Be patient and follow the steps. It will be worth it.

Chapter Two

What is Your Message?

2

WHAT IS YOUR MESSAGE?

Okay, here's another tough one: what is your message? What is the central idea behind your business? Two or three people can run the exact same business, whether it's a clothing line, a dry cleaners, a law practice, or selling a beauty product, and the message behind each of the businesses can be completely different for each one. It is vitally important to understand what your message is, what you're trying to say, and what you are trying to communicate to your prospective clients.

Take a few minutes and write a description of what your message is and what you want to get across to your audience. Think of it as a brief mission statement that helps define you and your business, giving you a clear vision of what it is you want to accomplish.

This isn't easy and the answers aren't always obvious. It may take some time soul searching. What is your message? It is important that your audience, clients, or patients realize that you are not just selling a product or a service, but that there is a message behind it.

I Want To Save The World

People have a tendency to get awfully bogged down with this message stuff. I'm not talking about anything profound or earth-shattering here. You're not answering that all-important question at the Miss America pageant. Just write a brief, simple, clarifying statement that describes what you offer. Your message might be that your product is as good as the competition, but less expensive. You offer a more individualized, personalized service. Your book teaches people to see things in a different light. Your product makes life easier for business people. It can be as basic as, "we offer our clients honest, hard work," to as revolutionary as, "this product is the newest of its kind and will change life as we know it." Are you the fastest, the most dependable, do you go the extra mile in the service you offer? What is it about how you do what you do that makes your business different?

Some businesses may have messages that are more broad-based, such as helping the community or healing the environment, whereas others will focus on offering better quality or giving up-to-the-minute information. There are as many messages as there are businesses. This isn't a moral issue, so don't get overwhelmed thinking that your message has to be some type of grandiose statement. This is a basic, practical matter.

**What is it that you offer that makes you special?
Why should your clients, patients or customers come to you
instead of your competitor down the block?**

Let's take this book as an example. My message is: I wanted to write a book that explains the immense power that effective media placement can have on a business or a career and gives the reader the tools with which to utilize this power to achieve success. My message, or primary objective, could have been to teach cardiologists in the state of New Jersey how to best use public relations to build a successful practice, or to show CEOs of Fortune 500 companies how to use public relations to reverse negative press, or to give a comprehensive overview of the history of public relations. Any one of those ideas would make for an interesting book, but none of them would be this book. Unless I knew precisely what my message was and what I wanted to accomplish by writing this book, I would never have been able to achieve my goal.

The list is endless, but the following are some fast, simple examples of messages:

· A clothing store that offers clients higher quality and better service than the competition.
· A physician who specializes in oncology and offers patients state-of-the-art treatment and diagnostic procedures.
· A nationwide computer software company that is on the cutting edge of the field and offers customers high quality, but less expensive, products.
· A day spa that features the latest massage and facial techniques and offers its clients a relaxing escape from their stressful lives.
· A new Internet company that creates exciting, effective Web pages and works with its customers to become Internet literate.
· A psychotherapist who authors a book on marriage and uses her years of experience in the field to outline tried-and-true steps to help her readers build stronger, happier, and more fulfilled relationships.

Selling Your Message

Your message may be more specific than these examples, but I want to emphasize that it need not be. Once you understand what your basic message is, you can begin to refine it. For example, if you are an auto dealer whose basic message is that you offer better service than the competition, the fact that you offer better service is your basic message. But that's just your starting point. Now you need to explain your message in a way that will interest the media and the public. It's not enough to simply say you give better service. How do you give better service? What do you offer that your competition doesn't? What unique services or benefits do you offer? Be specific. You are moving from the general, "we give better service," to the specific, "we offer a free shuttle service and a free oil change." It is the message that defines you, but the specifics that will sell your story.

Defining Your Target Market

Once you have defined and written your message, it's important to define your target market. Who is your audience? If you've developed a new anti-wrinkle cream and are marketing it to teenage boys, you'd better take another look at your strategy. You may have the best product in the world, but you've picked the wrong target audience, and it's not going to work. Believe me, this isn't an uncommon mistake; more businesses than you think have done everything right and gone belly up because they were targeting the wrong audience. This is an essential component of success. Know your prospective clientele. And don't let your ego or your preconceived ideas get in the way. If you have developed a product that you want to market to CEOs who earn over $100,000.00 a year, but your real market is junior high school students, you'd better learn that and learn it quickly.

For example, early on in my career I worked with a dentist who had written a book on various aspects of dentistry. The book was well done and contained information that would have probably been of interest to other dentists, but to no one else. The dentist was dead set on marketing his book to the general public, whereas his true market was a specialized niche market—other dentists. His perception of his target market was askew. He erroneously believed that because he found the information in his book both interesting and useful, everyone else would as well. I suggested that we pitch other dentistry-oriented stories that would interest the media. I tried to explain that if we were able to land him an interview on the newest in braces or teeth whitening, he could also discuss his book during the interview. But he would have none of it. He insisted that we pitch his book and his book only. I mistakenly allowed myself to go against my better judgement and agreed to pitch only his book. Well, we both learned our lesson the hard way. Although his book may have been perfect to promote to others in his profession, the general public was not his target market.

Be realistic about your business and your target market. Not every product or service has a huge market, but if you can define your market and effectively reach it, you're in business. Remember, just because you've devoted twenty years of your life to the world of hard-ware and find wrenches and sockets fascinating, don't automatically assume that everyone else does. They don't. This is a difficult but invaluable lesson to learn.

Finding Your Niche

Is your audience a mass market or a special niche audience? If it's a special niche audience, how is it defined: by age, by gender, by geo-graphical demographics? Are your customers primarily men or women, urban or rural? These are all extremely important questions. Do your homework. Take a look at your competitors and see how they market and whom they market to. I'm not recommending that you do expensive demographic testing or studies, just use some common sense and get rid of any preconceived ideas you have. Try to step out-side and look at your business as a disinterested onlooker. Although I believe that it is important to listen to your gut feeling, you have to walk a fine line, be realistic, be cautious, get feedback from others, weigh all the possibilities, and then make your decisions.

For example, let's say you've developed a new line of baby wear. Okay, who is your target market? Parents, and primarily mothers. Right off the bat, I'd say you could write off auto racing and golf-ori-ented publications as your primary target markets. Where do you reach mothers? The most obvious would be parent-and children-ori-ented publications (of which there are many), talk shows, local mag-azines, newspapers, TV and radio programs, and women's magazines. But study the women's magazines: are any of the articles or ads tar-geted towards parents of infants and toddlers? You want magazines that new mothers read. *Seventeen*, or *Sassy* magazine should probably not be on the top of your list.

Once you have defined your message, and your market, and nar-rowed your demographics, what now? You have done all of your pre-liminary work, work that most people tend to ignore. You have defined what you do, what your message is, and who your target mar-ket is. Now you are ready to start practicing the art which can change your business and your life. You're ready to learn to communicate your message not only to the person next door, but to hundreds, thousands, even millions of people across your city, throughout the country, and around the world. But first, answer one question: why do you deserve to promote yourself?

Chapter Three

Singing Your Praises and Staying on Key

3

SINGING YOUR PRAISES AND STAYING ON KEY

Why do you deserve to promote yourself? From childhood, most of us are taught that we should never beat our own drum (or toot our own horn, pick whatever instrument you like). We should never celebrate our abilities or publicly display our gifts or talents. It's just not a nice thing to do. It's not right. Come to think of it, it's downright immoral. The reasoning usually goes something like this: if you're good at what you do, that's enough. Your ability, capability, or uniqueness is its own reward, and you shouldn't bother the rest of us by telling us about it. I assume that this particular line of reasoning was foisted on the rest of us by some very insecure and frightened folk. If you feel this way, it's time to change your perspective. These are dangerous misconceptions that you have to put to rest. You not only can, you should tell people that you're good at your profession. You work hard, you offer quality, and you are doing the public a service by letting them know about your business.

For media magic to work, you have to work hard, do your best, offer quality, and believe in the quality of yourself and your work. If you don't believe in yourself, no amount of media coverage is going to help you. If you offer poor service, sell an inferior product, or seriously doubt the quality of your business and ability, steer clear of publicity. As I tell my clients, we can get them on the media, but once there, they have to deliver the goods. It all comes down to who they

17

are, the way they present themselves, and the quality of their business or service.

Constantly work on improving and perfecting what you do. Make your product or service the best it can be. Offer quality. If you do that, you have nothing to be embarrassed about. You may still feel some discomfort when it comes to singing your praises, but that will be because you're unused to hearing yourself praised, not because the praise is not warranted.

The Importance Of Beating Your Own Drum

Understand that although promoting yourself may seem a bit uncomfortable, it's not only warranted, it's necessary. Steven Spielberg, Donna Karan, Bill Gates, Martha Stewart—all these people excel in their field, but why is it you know them by name? Even Mother Theresa's publisher publicizes her book. They'd be foolish not to. What possible good is it to do quality work if no one is ever going to know about it?

Understand the importance of promoting yourself. If you believe what you do is important, then it is of equal importance to let others know about it, otherwise you're not serving your business, yourself, or the public. What good is it to offer a quality product, if no one is ever going to know it exists? What good is all your hard work, if it's kept a secret? You may be an expert at what you do, but if it is not in some way brought to the attention of others, your career or business will assuredly fail.

Start thinking like a business person, an entrepreneur, and a proud one at that. Promotion is an integral and extremely necessary part of any kind of business overview. People don't shy away when they hear that they need a business plan, an office, a phone, or business stationery, yet they cringe at the thought of promotion. *Effective publicity is as integral a part of your business as the service you offer or the materials you use.*

If you have trouble promoting yourself, keep in mind that your job is to get your message across. Your message is what you are working to promote. This isn't a beauty contest, but a campaign designed to educate and bring your message to the general public. Your message is important to promote. You want to reach the largest audience possible, and the media is the most effective and expedient way to do it.

The results of an effective media campaign can be remarkable. The ability to reach literally millions of people within a few hours is a very real form of magic, and the most powerful form of communication. **Always keep in mind that your purpose is to communicate**. Your objective is not to sell, preach, lecture or command, but to communicate. Communication is what it's all about.

You Never Know Who's Watching

What makes my business so fascinating is the unexpected. Media placement can result in totally surprising and unanticipated results. I always start a campaign with certain objectives in mind. I have a target market that I want to reach and I have some objective that I want to achieve. But because of the powerful nature of publicity, I have witnessed some amazing results that neither I nor my clients envisioned. I have had clients offered their own radio and TV shows after having been seen on the media. I've had clients offered positions in other companies, larger companies have offered buy-outs or mergers, and one client was offered complete financing on a new business venture after appearing on one talk show.

I'd love to say that I had intentionally masterminded it all, but I was as surprised as my clients when these offers and proposals came in. That's what makes it so fascinating. You never know who's watching or listening, and you never know where that last story or interview will lead you.

Chapter Four

The Marketing Game: Advertising vs. Media Placement

4

THE MARKETING GAME: ADVERTISING VS. MEDIA PLACEMENT

There are a variety of different ways to let the public know about your business, from buying a multi-million dollar commercial spot during the Super Bowl and placing a full-page ad in *USA Today*, to passing out flyers at the local mall and standing in front of your office with a blow horn.

The primary ways to reach your target market include advertising, public relations, and direct marketing. It's important to understand how these various forms of marketing work and how they differ. Although the following is a basic thumbnail sketch, it will hopefully give you a rudimentary understanding of these forms of marketing and how they work. But keep in mind, public relations is my business. I've witnessed some amazing PR success stories, for both companies with big budgets and individuals working on a shoestring. So, I admit—I'm biased.

Advertising

Ah yes, advertising. You know, those TV commercials you flip past and those print ads you skip over. Advertising is basically a paid endorsement. Advertising can be placed on TV or radio, in a magazine or newspaper, or on a billboard or bus bench. For many businesses, advertising is essential. It can be a significant component of an overall marketing program. Advertising lets the public know who you are, what you're selling, where you're located, and your business's best features. Advertising can help sway a potential client or customer your way, who is perhaps considering buying a similar product or using a competitor's service. If you have enough funds, you can control where and when your ad will run, as well as how big it will be, what it will say, and how it will look.

But advertising has its down sides. Advertising lacks credibility. The public is sophisticated enough to realize that an ad or commercial is a paid endorsement. You are buying ad space or commercial time in order to tell the world just how wonderful you and your business really are. If you sell tires and run an ad saying you have the best quality, prices, and service in town, this is what's expected— what else are you going to say?

Advertising is generally a very expensive proposition. An effective advertising campaign requires repetition, which means you not only need to repeat the ad, but you need to repeat the process of writing out a check to pay for the ad. You need to be committed to a campaign in order to reach your target market. Utilized properly, advertising can be very effective. There are companies who strictly rely on advertising to build their business. But keep in mind, the advertising industry is run by advertising sales people, whose primary job is to convince you that you need to advertise. If advertising works for you, stick with it. If not, look at other options. In my opinion, millions of dollars are spent on advertising each year by businesses who advertise only because they have been expertly convinced that they should.

Publicity/Media Placement

Although people have a tendency to lump advertising and publicity together, they are extremely different animals. Advertising pays the bills for a newspaper or TV program. Ads and commercials generate the funds that keeps the media going. Ads are the reason that magazines, newspapers, news programs, or talk shows exist. But be honest, how often do you skip through the pages of ads in a magazine to get to the articles or channel-surf in order to avoid TV commercials? I know I do.

The reason that effective media placement is so powerful is that it makes *your story* an integral part of that magazine article or TV program; it makes *you* a part of the reason that John (and Joan) Q. Public have picked up that magazine or turned on that program. Why? Because you become the story. You have sidestepped the advertising section of the media and jumped to the editorial section. You are a part of the reason that readers have bought the magazine or viewers have turned on the program. Unlike an advertiser, you are not paying for your article or interview. In fact, *all of those individuals and businesses who are buying ad or commercial space are actually paying the costs for your story to run.*

Why Be The Story?

You have been picked by the editor of a newspaper, or the segment producer of a TV program to become part of a story in which you are to be featured or quoted. The media found you important enough to be interviewed and to represent your field. But why do you want to be the story? What good does that do you? Quite a lot. Let's take a look at the top three benefits media placement can bring to you and your business.

1. **Prominence By Association** —Let's say you are being featured on an evening news segment; your interview could be placed in between an interview with the President of the United States and a feature on the newest medical breakthrough. What difference does that make? You've heard of guilt by association? This is importance and prominence by association. It is said that we are judged by the company we keep. You are now in the company of the newsworthy, and because of your association, you have suddenly leaped ahead of your competition.

2) **Mass Communication**—By being featured in the media, your business, service, or product will reach (depending on whether the

story is local, regional, or national) hundreds, thousands, and possibly millions of people. You will not be viewed as a hard sell, as another ad to ignore, but as a communicator of information. You and your message will enter homes and businesses, not as an ad or commercial, but as a news story.

3) **Validation**—Anyone who reads, sees, or hears you interviewed or featured in the media will perceive you as an expert. Instead of being viewed as someone who is trying to sell them a product or service, you will be perceived as an authority. When people seek you out, they will be seeking you out as a specialist, as someone whom the media deems important enough to be featured in the press. You have avoided spending thousands of dollars in advertising and have gained something no amount of advertising could ever buy you—credibility.

Publicity vs. Advertising

It's important to comprehend how vastly different public relations is from advertising. Used correctly, advertising can help bring you a fast response. If you're having a fire sale, you want to advertise. You can put an ad out in a day, control what it says, and pick where and when it will run.

Media placement should never be viewed as a quick fix; it is a cumulative process. It needs to be an ongoing part of your business plan. It involves placing story after story, segment after segment. You slowly build yourself as an expert in your field, as someone whom the media seeks out, and as someone who is presented to the general public as newsworthy.

The purpose and effect of media placement are quite different from those of advertising. Advertising is not known for its subtlety. Every advertiser is competing with every other advertiser to grab the public's attention. Some will yell and some will whisper, but the bottom line remains the same: "buy ours." Although advertising has become increasingly sophisticated, it still is and will always remain a variation on one basic theme. Stripped bare of all the high-tech effects, at its roots, all advertising is still a version of the barker at the circus. "Ladies and Gentlemen, boys and girls, come on in and buy this product."

Publicity's Bad PR

Media placement is much more subtle. When utilizing media placement, you too want them to come on in and buy your product, but you also have a very different objective. You want to educate, you want to communicate with the public. I don't think that I can emphasize this point strongly enough. Publicity has bad PR. It is known for its fluff and hype, for the sleight-of-hand work done by high-paid spin doctors, and, believe me, all of that exists. But the glitter and flash isn't all there is. There is a whole other side to publicity. What makes media placement effective is that it educates, it gives the public information on a particular topic or field that they otherwise wouldn't have access to. Let's look at a couple of examples.

We represented a physician who was working on a new cancer drug and was in the midst of clinical tests. The first series had been quite promising. He was looking for patients with a certain type of cancer who were interested in participating in the study. He received hundreds of calls after a local TV interview ran, from people wanting to find out more information. These people would never have been aware of the study, if it had not been for the interview they saw.

How about a couple of examples that aren't quite so serious? A client, who is a skin care expert and has created her own make-up line, appeared on a TV segment teaching consumers how to buy cosmetics for less. The piece explained how to read and understand labels and how to shop for high quality, yet inexpensive products.

Another client, who is a fitness expert, was interviewed by a major magazine on exercise and pregnancy. The article was an educational and informative piece on the types of exercises that expectant mothers should and should not do.

All of these pieces highlighted and focused on the client, but they also educated. By watching the interviews or reading the article, the public came away with something. The pieces were informative and (hopefully) added to the quality of the viewers' or readers' lives, Which is precisely why media placement is so powerful. Done correctly, it educates, instructs, entertains, and whets the public's appetite to know more, to make an appointment, or to visit a store.

Once again it comes down to communication. You are not only building the image of an expert, of someone whom both the media and the public turn to for information and advice, you are communicating with and educating the public.

The Road Not Taken

You have a specific budget for marketing. You can either designate it for advertising or public relations. What should you do? My first suggestion is to take another look at your budget and see if there is a way to do a little of each. But if your budget is such that you have to make a choice, I'd start with publicity. The expense is not nearly as great. You can prime the pump with some well-placed stories, and once your cash flow begins to increase you can expand your marketing budget to include advertising.

Let's look at an example of how advertising and media placement differ. You're interested in buying a new car and just happen to be thumbing through a copy of *Fortune* magazine. You come across an ad for a car. The ad is pretty and glossy. It is a photo of a beach scene at sunset. The colors are more beautiful than those in real life. The photo has an attractive man and woman dressed in sophisticated evening attire standing by the car, which is parked in the sand, just beyond the reach of the aquamarine waves. The copy tells you that this car is the best thing to hit this country since sliced bread and that you can't exist another day without running out and buying it. The photo tells you that if you do buy the car, you will be transported to that idyllic beach scene. You live in Cincinnati, Ohio, it is the dead of winter, and damn if that idyllic marine scene doesn't look inviting.

You continue to look through the magazine and come upon an article on the year's best cars. The article mentions a certain car (not the one you saw in the ad), and touts the car as being one of the most efficient, best-built, and luxurious cars on the market. The article is simple, direct, and informative and is written by an expert in the automotive field. Which do you think will have the most impact on you, the ad or the article?

My guess is, after the Caribbean fantasies die down, the article will have the greatest impact on you. Why? Credibility. The ad may give you some basic information, but it primarily offers you a fantasy. The car is bright and shiny. It is parked on an empty, pristine beach. The sun is setting in the background. There is a sexy, tanned couple, in evening attire no less, standing by the immaculate, gleaming car. Nine times out of ten, you're not buying the car, you're buying the scene—the fantasy.

The article, on the other hand, raises your comfort level. You have been given objective information on the car's effectiveness and quality. An expert has kicked the tires for you and given you a clean report. You have moved from fantasy to reality. The car featured in the ad may seem more sexy or romantic, but the one spotlighted in the article becomes real. Not only is it luxurious, it is dependable, efficient, and reliable. Remember, it's 20 below outside, reliable is important. It is this type of credibility or validation that cannot be bought in the form of an ad.

As I mentioned, media placement is also much more cost-effective than advertising. If you are on a tight budget, an ongoing advertising campaign can drain your finances in no time. But, although it is less costly, to be effective, media placement takes time, work, and creativity. Because it is a cumulative process (and I can't stress this enough) it takes persistence, inventiveness, and patience.

Along with public relations and advertising, direct marketing, mailing out brochures, information, or flyers to a target market, is another valuable way to reach your market. Although direct marketing can be a very effective tool, it is more akin to advertising than it is to public relations.

No Guarantees

Neither advertising nor media placement can guarantee a return. Advertising can guarantee what an ad will say, where it will appear, and when and where it will run, but there are no guarantees that that ad will generate customers, sales, patients or clients.

With publicity as well, there are no guarantees. When prospective new clients demand that I offer them a guarantee, I explain that the only guarantee I can offer is my track record. I can show media I've placed in the past and give an honest assessment of whether or not I believe I can put together a successful campaign for the clients. If a public relations company guarantees you specific placement or a successful campaign, I suggest you start looking for the exit. There are no guarantees.

No one can guarantee you success, but you can certainly prepare yourself for it. New clients often want me to promise them that within two weeks I'll have them on *60 Minutes* or in *Time* magazine. I have worked on campaigns that have moved this quickly, but, believe me, that's not the norm. Each campaign has a life of its own, and you just can't predict how it's going to go. Nor is it possible to determine exactly how long it will take to start placing stories. I work on a six-month initial contract, so that it gives us some time to put together an effective campaign. We have been able to place some clients on national shows and in magazines within the first week; with other clients we have worked for months before landing the first story. That's why patience is perhaps the most important aspect of an effective campaign. If you pull the plug after one, two, or even three months of no press, you'll never know what a real campaign could have accomplished.

For example, we worked on one campaign for three months, with little to show for our efforts. Needless to say, by the end of the third month, our client was more than a bit nervous. He had paid us a retainer fee for three months and had received very little in return. But he stuck with it. We formulated a new direction for the campaign, wrote some new releases, and by the end of the fifth month we had placed stories on *CNN* and *Leeza*, as well as in *Newsweek The Los*

Angeles Times, and various other media outlets. That's why it is so important to be committed to a campaign. If the client had stopped in three months, the entire campaign would have been for naught. If you give the media good stories and you're professional, creative, and tenacious, eventually, you will get placement.

That's why it is so vitally important to know what you're doing before you start. You want to make sure you're not just spinning your wheels and doing what you *think* is publicity. You can waste a great deal of time and money sending out literature that is immaterial or inappropriate, or making phone calls that turn out to be more of a nuisance than a help to the media. If you don't bother to learn how to implement a professional, effective publicity campaign, chances are you'll end up wasting your time and money. But before we get to the nuts and bolts of media placement, answer one more important question: where do you want to go?

Chapter Five

Where are You Going?

5

WHERE ARE YOU GOING?

Let's do a fast recap. You now understand what you do, know what publicity aka media placement is, as well as the difference between publicity and advertising, know your message, and defined your target media. Time to jump in and start the magic, right? Almost. One final question: *where do you want to go?*

Do you want to be in newspapers or on TV just for the fun of it, or do you have a specific objective in mind? I can't emphasize how important it is to have clearly defined your goals before you start your campaign. These are objectives that you must decide for yourself.

Ask yourself the following questions:

· Where do you want publicity to take you and your business?
· How big do you want your business to grow?
· At what rate do you want your business to grow?
· What do you want to accomplish through your publicity campaign?
· What target market do you want to reach?
· How do you want to be perceived by the media?
· What are your short-term and long-term media goals?

When I began in the field, I assumed that, before clients decided to hire me, they had outlined their goals, knew where they wanted their business to go, and knew what objectives they wanted to achieve. I was wrong. I now have prospective clients clearly outline their goals before we start a campaign. I used to spend the bulk of my initial consultation with clients selling myself and my service. Now the bulk of the time is spent finding out not only who the prospective client is, but what he or she wants to accomplish and what objectives need to be met. The bottom line is, if you don't know where you're going, how will you know when you've arrived?

For example, let's say a veterinarian based in Boston, who has one office and has neither books nor products to sell, decides to launch a publicity campaign around her practice. Her primary objectives are to build her practice and to eventually open another practice across town. We know what she does and know her objectives, so we can begin to outline what type of campaign would be most effective for her. In her case, regional press would probably be a waste of time. Not many people from Florida or Montana are going to fly Fido in to see her in Boston, and since she has neither products nor books that she can sell, there is little benefit in concentrating on regional press. Now, if she had the newest nutritional supplement for Tabby or had written the definitive book on training your dog, that would be a different story. She could use regional radio and TV shows and newspaper stories to help sell her products. But, whereas this particular veterinarian would be wasting her time doing regional press, both local and national press would be invaluable to her. Local press would help bring in clients and national press would help feed the local press.

These decisions are crucial and have to be made early on. You need a game plan, but the only way you can implement an effective plan is by understanding your objectives. You want to avoid appearing on national TV shows talking about products that are still in the development stage or about books you have yet to write. You need to be prepared. Put your media campaign in order, prepare, but don't move forward until you are ready.

Long-Term Plans

This is the point where you have to decide not only what media is applicable to your business, but also how you want to utilize your media and where you want it to take your business or career. Stating that you want media to bring in more clients, customers, or patients isn't good enough. Study your business plan. *How can media placement help you meet your objectives? Do you want to increase your business by a third in one year? Do you want to open another store or branch? Do you want to take a product national? What are your long term goals?* Without such goals, you have no way to measure the success of the campaign.

Keep your eye on the long term. Remember, media placement is a long-term, cumulative process. If you are only looking five weeks or even six months down the line, broaden your scope. Write down your short-term and long-term objectives. Where does media placement fit in? How can the magic of the media help you to achieve your objectives? Seek advice from others. But don't let someone else answer these questions for you. These are question only you can answer.

Finally, don't come up with a plan that has you appearing on *Oprah, The Tonight Show*, or in *Time Magazine* and *The Wall Street Journal* within the first two months of your campaign. That's not a plan, that's fantasy. There is one particular client I work with who has been featured in almost all the major national TV programs and magazines. He's been featured in many of them several times, but these interviews did not come about overnight. His success is the result of an ongoing five-year campaign. This isn't to say that it takes five years to launch an effective campaign, but to emphasize the fact that, if you are going to launch an effective media campaign, be committed to the future. *Media placement is not a luxury, but a necessary, powerful, key marketing tool. Think of it as being an essential part of your business.*

Chapter Six

Learning Alchemy

6

LEARNING ALCHEMY

Okay. Now it's time to learn *The Alchemy of Success* and start the magic.

The Press Release aka Tell Me
Your Story In One Page Or Less

Ah, the infamous press release. What is it? Traditionally, a press release is a one-to five-page document that tells your story. Unlike a letter, there is no salutation, nor is the release personalized or written to a particular person. It is a general document you can use for the different media. There are some set-in-stone, very specific guidelines to press releases, such as covering the who, what, where, and when information, adhering to the press release format, and keeping it double-spaced. Personally, I probably break more of these set-in-stone rules than I keep. Most press releases are horribly, terrifically boring. They are dry, and chock-full of dull, tedious facts, or they are overly cute.

Since I concentrate solely on media placement, as far as I am concerned, there is only one purpose for a press release—to interest the media, to interest editors, writers, or producers in my clients and their stories. And that ain't necessarily easy. The media is inundated with press releases, and most are filled with information that is unusable or inappropriate. Don't become known as one of the monotonous release senders. Once you're identified as part of the "don't bother" lot, your releases will be tossed in the circular file as soon as they arrive.

Cutting Your Trailer

I have a hard-and-fast rule at my company that press releases cannot exceed one page. I will sacrifice double-spacing in order to come up with a one-page release. But, you argue, you have so much interesting and important information to impart. You couldn't possibly say all that you wanted to in one page. You're right. So don't. Only give them the headlines, the teasers. Imagine that you're cutting a trailer for an upcoming movie. You're not concerned with trying to let the audience see the entire film. Your job is to interest the public enough to plunk down their money to see the movie. It's the same with your press release. You want your release to act as a teaser; you want to interest the media, grab their attention.

You Think Editors Have Time To Read?

Even though you may be sending your release to a magazine editor, the ironic truth is that the editor has no time to read. He or she is busy trying to get work done. If you send a four-or five-page release, no matter how impeccable it looks or how perfect the grammar or form is—*no one's going to want, or have the time, to read it.*

It all comes down to your pitch, your hook: is it interesting, exciting? Will it meet the media's needs? If not, don't mail it, fax it, or let it leave your place. Start again. Do your homework. Put yourself in the media's place and come up with a hook or story idea that will grab their attention.

Remember, you're not trying to reinvent the wheel or come up with a completely unique idea or pitch. There are no completely unique ideas. You are trying to come up with usable, interesting story ideas. Some of them may be different or unique, others will be ordinary and prosaic. But an ordinary story can be a good one if presented the right way.

For example, let's say you own a hair salon, and it's getting near the end of the year. Write a "New Look For The New Year" release in which you outline how you can give clients a new, personalized look to start the New Year with a fresh start. You might even want to invite the media to follow a client through the before, during, and after process. This way the media comes away with a visually interesting holiday story, and you come away with an effective piece which establishes you as an innovator in your field.

If you are announcing a new product, make sure that the information coincides with the product's availability. Include a sample along with the press information that you send to the media, as well as information on how to order the product.

Headlines, Headlines, Headlines

Make sure to keep your press release tight and concise—no rambling—and remember, think in terms of headlines. There is a reason that *USA Today, People Magazine* and *MTV* are successful. They give us quick, easy-to-digest stories. Ours is a society that likes the fast-food approach to information. Package it nicely, make it interesting, make it short, don't take a lot of our time and we'll read it, watch it, or listen to it. Be smart, and use that same approach when pitching story ideas to the media.

Don't fool yourself into thinking that because you're only writing a one-page release, you can knock it out in half an hour. A good press release can take quite a bit of time to write. As with all writing, the hardest and most important part is the editing. Your first attempt may be three or four pages long. Don't worry about it. Write your first draft without any concern for space, punctuation, or style. Concentrate on the facts and information. Once you have the basic story down, start editing it, cutting it down. Can you say something in a sentence instead of a paragraph? Do you really need to give all that information? It's not easy. Write in headlines—*you are not giving them the story—you are giving them the idea.* Don't try to rush it. Take your time. Put it aside for a couple of days, then reevaluate it. Can it be improved? I've spent days on certain one-page releases. Remember, think in terms of headlines. You're not trying to tell the whole story, you're looking to grab the reader's attention.

And, speaking of headlines, always make sure to start your release with a headline that is centered. I always bold my headline and make it a larger point size than the rest of the copy. What makes for a good headline? Anything that will make them read on. You only have about seven or eight words to work with, so it can take some time to come up with the right one. Sometimes it's fun to be clever or use alliteration, but be careful, you don't want to be too cute. Be imaginative, not precious. Make it interesting.

For example, let's say you want to promote a new skin care product that contains vitamin C. You could come up with a headline that reads:

NEW SKIN CARE PRODUCT NOW AVAILABLE

or you could write a release that reads:

BEAUTY IN THE KEY OF C

The first headline actually gives the reader more information than the second, but chances are the second headline will do a better job of catching the reader's eye. What does "beauty in the key of C" mean? That's exactly what you want the reader to ask, and the only way to find out is to read the release.

Breaking The Rules

Most experts will suggest that you stick with the traditional press release form and put your name, address, and contact information on the top. Don't. *The first few lines of your release may be all that gets read.* Don't sacrifice that all-important space to mundane information. Come up with an interesting headline that is centered on the page, and immediately start with your story. Keep the information on how to contact you at the bottom of the page. If your story interests them, believe me, they'll call, no matter where you put your number.

Although I am suggesting that you break some of the common press release rules, don't try to be novel or unconventional simply for the sake of being different. The changes I suggest are based on practical observations. Too often we stick to a form simply because that's the way it's been done before. If there is a practical, advantageous reason to do something different, do it.

On the other hand, don't be different simply to be different. In other words, don't use oversized paper, or unconventional script, or write cryptic or convoluted sentences just to try to differentiate yourself from the rest of the pack. Chances are, it will only work against you. You want to catch the media's eye, but you don't want to shock or startle. Keep the release clean and easy-to-read, and remember, no amount of inventiveness will make up for the lack of a good hook or story.

At the bottom of the page, make sure to let the media know who you are and how they can get in contact with you; have your phone number and contact person clearly listed.

Stand back and look at your release with an objective eye. If you knew nothing about your business or product, and you saw your release, would it make you want to learn more about the topic? Would it pique your interest? If not, you're headed in the wrong direction. Bounce it off other people, get feedback. Don't send it out until it says exactly what you want it to say, in the way you want to say it. And never, ever, ever let it be longer than one page.

To Write Or Not To Write

If writing intimidates you, or you just don't feel you can put down your ideas in the way you would like, hire someone to do it for you. It doesn't have to be expensive. Believe me, there are a lot of hungry writers around. Look in the paper or ask around at copy centers or colleges. Find a writer you're comfortable with, one that understands what you're trying to say and can put those ideas down in an interesting manner.

If you're writing the release yourself, make sure you have someone proof it. Even if you have to pay someone, it's worth it. Don't ever let a release go out before it has been proofed for mistakes by someone other than yourself.

Style, Grammar, Spelling And All That Other Fun Stuff

Remember, content is just one part of your release. The form, look, and style is every bit as important.

Before sending out a release, double-check the following:

> Is the form correct? Is the grammar and spelling correct? Is the release clean and mistake-free? If your release looks sloppy, if it's filled with spelling and grammatical errors, or if it's crammed with hard-to-read small print, no one is going to read it. You might have written a great release, but if you don't take the care to present it properly, it's useless. Make sure to avoid dot matrix printers, poor copies, and carbon copies. Also, don't try to be overly cute or fancy. Keep your typeface clean, simple, and easy to read. Include the most important information in the first paragraph. Send a personalized cover letter with the release. Make sure your release is relevant, timely, and, most of all, offers the media a story. This next one may seem obvious, but people forget to include it every day: have you included your phone number along with your name, or the name of the person that the media should contact?

Make sure your release is as easy to read as possible, and keep a lot of white space on the page; use bullets, boxes, anything to break up the page so that it's not just a block of words that no one is going to read. Most people will suggest that you double-space, but if you have to choose between double-spacing a release and writing a one-page release, keep it single-spaced. Just make sure to keep your typeface at least twelve point. Don't send out a release that's a thick block of words—go for light instead of dense.

The Press Release Review

The following is a quick checklist to review before sending your releases out.

Remember to:

- Define your message.
- Keep your press release to one page. That is law.
- Keep your release clean, crisp and easy-to-read.
- Sell the story, not yourself.
- Study the type of stories that the various media outlets need.
- Pitch stories that meet the media's needs.
- Modify your release to fit the needs of the various media outlets you are pitching.
- Confirm the address and fax number of the media outlet before sending information.
- Mail or fax your information to the appropriate media contact.
- If you are announcing an event, be sure to include the place, time, and date.
- Be creative, but keep your release simple, concise and to the point.
- Have someone else proof your release for grammatical and spelling errors.
- Be sure to cover all of the who, what, where, and when information.
- Think in terms of headlines.
- List your name and contact number at the bottom of the page.
- Position yourself as a resource, not a salesperson.
- Allow plenty of time for your release to arrive.
- Keep the release clean and mistake-free.

And Never:

- Use carbon paper, or print a release on a dot matrix printer.
- Send out a sloppy release.

· Send your release out until you are completely satisfied with it.
· Cram it with hard-to-read small print.
· Be overly cute or fancy.

A Quick Media Review

Television

Remember to target your local media including cable, community and college TV. Keep in mind that community-oriented early morning news programs and morning talk shows will often focus on one topic of community programming. When sending a release to television news programs, allow three days to one week lead time. When sending information to talk shows, allow at least two to four weeks. Study the last ten minutes of broadcast on the local news. That time slot usually features soft news and human interest stories.

Magazines

Look for special-interest publications dedicated to covering news in your field. These are magazines that are devoted to one particular field or area. When pitching a story to a weekly magazine send your information out one month to six weeks in advance. If pitching a monthly magazine make sure to get your information to the editor a minimum of three months in advance. If you are pitching a Christmas-oriented story, send it in August. Keep magazine guides in mind as potential media outlets. These are tourist-oriented publications that are usually distributed in hotels and in some restaurants.

Newspapers

When pitching the local newspapers, develop a local hook that is community-oriented. If you are pitching a daily or metro newspaper make sure to allow a minimum of two weeks. Although there have been countless stories predicting the death of newspapers, remember over one half of the country receives a daily paper. This is an extremely powerful, multi-billion dollar industry. When pitching a weekly or biweekly paper allow a minimum of three weeks. Offer to write articles for trade, community-based or local publications, free of charge. Also keep in mind ethnic papers which are rapidly growing around the country. Never overlook club newsletters, church bulletins, business association newsletters and small newspapers.

Radio

Pitch a story to a radio program at least two weeks in advance. Many radio shows have call-in formats, so be prepared to answer a variety of questions. If you have an 800 number, make sure and ask the producer if you can give it out over the air. Also make sure and leave your phone number with the station to give out to listeners who call in for information. If you have call waiting, remember to disconnect it before conducting an interview.

Newswire Services

Newswire services such as AP, UPI and Ryder gather information and provide stories to other media. The stories are written by the service's reporters and transmitted to newsrooms around the country. Newswire services also have a daybook, which list the day's newsworthy events. When pitching a story to a wire service make sure to send your information a minimum of two weeks in advance.

The Internet

An internet page will establish a presence for you and your company in cyberspace. Charges for basic home sites vary from fifty dollars to thousands of dollars depending on whom you hire and on how elaborate you want your page to be. A good net page will be visually interesting, entertaining and educational. There are said to be over 30 million people on the net, which you can potentially reach without sending a letter or sending a fax. The down side is you're never sure if you're reaching anyone. As the Internet grows and matures it will become more and more consequential. At present, it is an important tool to help further establish your presence and visibility, but in many ways I think that the NET's image still outweighs its usefulness.

The Press Tour

A press tour is generally of value for people who want to establish themselves within their field, have written a book, or have a nationally available product. A tour can be grueling and takes an awful lot of preparation. It is a way to gain greater awareness, to establish yourself as a corporate spokesperson and to help promote a book or product. A press tour takes planning and expertise. It is not something you just decide to do. An extensive tour can be quite expensive. It is best to organize a tour through a public relations company.

Announcing a Product

If you are announcing a new product, make sure that the information coincides with the product's availability. Include a photo and a sample along with the press information that you send to the media and information on how to order the product

Video News Releases

Another type of release is the video news release. These are professionally produced video tapes that you can send to the various TV outlets. A video news release is an expensive proposition and can run into the thousands of dollars. Don't confuse a video news release with a promotional tape or video of one of your TV appearances. It is a polished, ready-to-air piece. You pay for all of the production costs and give it free of charge to the media. They then decide whether to run it or not. If you are to have any chance of having your VNR run, it must be not only high-quality, it must also be newsworthy. Unless you have the funds and find an experienced company to produce and deliver the video news releases, I'd suggest you pass on this one.

Press Conferences

It's important to know when to hold a press conference. If you think that a press conference is the way to go, nine times out of ten you're going to be wrong. Although there are many types of press conferences, they are primarily utilized to give the media more information on breaking news stories or when a celebrity or well-known person is making a statement. Countless other types of press conferences are announced, but few receive any coverage. Politics and press conferences do go together. The only times we've used press conferences have been for various politicians that we've represented.

If you are going to hold a press conference, hold it in the mid-morning. The later in the day you hold it, the less media you will draw because of deadline scheduling conflicts. In my experience most press conferences are ineffective, because the story or pitch usually does not warrant a press conference. Try to think like the media, play devil's advocate with yourself. If you were a harried producer or editor, and were pitched a story on your proposed press conference, would it be of interest to you? If the answer is no, forget going the press conference route. Reframe the hook and pitch it as a regular story.

Announcing An Event

If you are announcing an event, or your information is time sensitive, be sure to have *For Immediate Release* at the top of the page (I suggest you put it on all of your releases.) Have you answered the who, what, where, and when questions? Have you included the day and time of the event, along with whether it's a.m. or p.m., and the time zone (Eastern, Pacific, etc.) Have you included the exact, full address of the event including city and state?

Before sending out a release, make sure you're pitching a story that will be of interest to the media, one that meets the media's needs. *And remember, be concise, keep it to one page. That's law.*

The following are two sample press releases based on this book. The first gives you all of the information you need. In fact it gives too much information. The second release gives the necessary information, but also breaks up the page visually and offers the media some basic story ideas.

Example 1—Press Release

For Immediate Release.

Anthony Mora Communications, Inc.
12304 Santa Monica Blvd., Suite 300
Los Angeles, CA 90025
Phone: (310) 207-6615, Fax: (310) 207-8380
Contact: Anthony Mora

The Alchemy of Success

Anthony Mora, president of Anthony Mora Communications, Inc., began his writing career as a music journalist for *US*, *Rolling Stone*, *Buzz*, *Playboy Publications* and other local and national publications. He also served as the editor-in-chief of two national magazines. In 1985, he left journalism to start Anthony Mora Communications. Anthony and his company have been featured in *The New York Times* and *Elle*, as well as on *CNN*, *E!*, *Extra*, and other media.

Anthony Mora's book, *The Alchemy of Success: Marketing Your Company/Career Through The Power Of The Media For Achieving Unlimited Success*, is a one-of-a-kind, step-by-step book on how to define goals and utilize the power of the media to achieve success. Whether you are starting a business, have developed a product, or are offering a service, the information and tools taught are indispensable.

Practical and user friendly, *The Alchemy of Success* can be utilized by heads of major corporations, small business owners, and entrepreneurs, as well as by victims of downsizing who are starting over. The book outlines how anyone can use *The Alchemy of Success* to build their businesses, launch their companies, and create their own success stories. Unlike any other form of marketing, publicity can help establish you as an expert in your field, and showcase your business, talent, or product, locally, nationally, and internationally. With effective public relations and media placement, you become the news.

Anthony Mora Communications Inc. has placed clients in a wide range of local, national and international media venues, including:

Time, *Newsweek*, *Today*, *CBS This Morning*, *CBS Evening News*, *People*, *US*, *Entertainment Tonight*, *20/20*, *Vogue*, *Fox News*, *KCAL*, *KTLA*, *KNBC*, *KCBS*, *Geraldo*, *USA Today*, *Star*, *Oprah*, *The London Times*, *The New York Times*, *The Los Angeles Times*, *Allure*, *Self*, and various other media outlets.

Anthony Mora Communications Inc. represents a wide range of clients. Clients have included: *Governor Jerry Brown's Presidential Campaign*, *Holly Hunter*, *Rachel Perry Cosmetics*, and *Gramercy Films*. The firm has worked with a number of authors and publishers, including: *Simon & Schuster*, *Hearst Books*, *Avon*, *Citadel Press*, and *Health Communications*.

Anthony Mora began his writing career as a music journalist for *US*, *Rolling Stone*, *Buzz*, *Playboy Publications*, and other local and national publications. After a short stint as an artist's manager, Anthony returned to the magazine arena as the editor-in-chief of *Impression* magazine, an English-language, Hispanic-oriented publication. The magazine, which featured such authors as *Octavio Paz*, *Carlos Fuentes*, *Gabriel Marcia Marquez* and *Carlos Casteneda*, focused on the arts, literature and entertainment. After about a year, Anthony left *Impression* to work as editor-in-chief of *Excel* magazine, an entertainment and lifestyle-oriented publication.

He left *Excel* to start Phillips & Mora Entertainment, a public relations company, which ventured into video and eventually film production. Anthony left the video and film production world and started Anthony Mora Communications, a media placement company.

Anthony Mora Communications, Inc. develops media material and organizes a comprehensive public relations campaign, which includes TV, magazines, newspapers, and radio.

For Further Information Contact:
Anthony Mora Communications, Inc. (310) 207-6615

Example 1—Cover Letter:

The Gotham Gazette
Attn.: Mr. Jack Newsman, Editor
0000 Gotham Place
Gotham City, Gotham 00000

Dear Mr. Newsman,

Enclosed please find information on my new book, *The Alchemy of Success, Marketing Your Company/Career Through The Power Of The Media For Achieving Unlimited Success*, for your consideration.
Please call if you have any questions or need further information.
I look forward to hearing from you.

Sincerely,

Anthony Mora,
Anthony Mora Communications, Inc.
AM:kat

Example 2—Press Release

For Immediate Release:

The Alchemy of Success

Why is media exposure the most powerful marketing tool available? Simple. What makes a business successful? Referrals—word of mouth. What if there was a way of magnifying the word of mouth effect? What if, in a matter of days, weeks, or months, you could broadcast your referrals to hundreds, thousands, or possibly millions of people? That's magic! And that's what the *Alchemy Of Success: Marketing Your Company/Career Through The Power Of The Media For Achieving Unlimited Success* is all about.

The Alchemy of Success Addresses Such Topics As:

- THE TEN BIGGEST MEDIA MISTAKES •
- THE IMPACT PR HAS ON THE MEDIA •
- MEETING THE MEDIA'S NEEDS •
- UNIQUE PR SUCCESS STORIES •
- MASTERING THE ART OF SOUND BYTES •
- THE PRESS KIT MYTH •
- HOW TO AVOID THE BIGGEST MEDIA MISTAKES •

Written by public relations expert, Anthony Mora, *The Alchemy of Success* is a one-of-a-kind, step-by-step book on how to define goals and utilize the power of the media to achieve success. The book outlines how anyone can master the power of the media to create success, wealth, and happiness.

A former journalist and magazine editor, Anthony Mora has owned his public relations firm for over ten years. His clients have appeared on *60 Minutes*, *Today* and *Oprah*, as well as in *Newsweek*, *The Wall Street Journal* and *Vogue*.

Whether you are starting a business, have developed a product, or are offering a service, the information and tools taught are indispensable. Practical and user friendly, *The Alchemy of Success* can be utilized by heads of major corporations, small business owners, and entrepreneurs, as well as by victims of downsizing who are starting over.

For Further Information Contact:
Anthony Mora Communications, Inc. (310) 207-6615

Example 2—Cover Letter

The Gotham Gazette
Attn.: Mr. Jack Newsman, Editor
0000 Gotham Place
Gotham City, Gotham 00000

Dear Mr. Newsman,

Not long ago, *Esquire* magazine ran a story on America's newest female film star. After the piece ran, the woman highlighted in the article was inundated with letters from adoring fans and offers from film studios. The payoff—it was a fabricated story. There was no such actress.

No one knows better than an editor the power and impact that an article or segment can have. A story or feature can virtually create a celebrity overnight or help launch a struggling company.

The following is information on my book, *The Alchemy Of Success: Marketing Your Company/Career Through The Power Of The Media For Achieving Unlimited Success*. It is a one-of-a-kind, step-by-step book on how to define goals and utilize the power of the media to achieve success. A former journalist and magazine editor, I have owned my company, Anthony Mora Communications, Inc. for over ten years. Our clients have appeared on countless media outlets, including *60 Minutes*, *Today*, and *Oprah*, as well as in *Newsweek*, *The Wall Street Journal*, and *Vogue*.

Please give me a call if you have any questions or need further information.

Sincerely,

Anthony Mora
Anthony Mora Communications, Inc.
AM: kat

Release #1

Both are press releases. The first one actually tells you a heck of a lot more than the second, but it's too long, too boring, and there are no ideas to work with. And look how far you have to read before there are any details about the book. The media doesn't need or want that much information. It's overkill. Once a particular media outlet is interested, you can follow-up with more information, but wait until you have their attention. The cover letter that accompanies the first release is dry, boring, and offers no information. It's a wasted page.

Release #2

The second release is one page, concise, pinpoints what the book is about, and highlights some specific topics and story ideas.

The cover letter that accompanies the second release begins with an anecdotal story that illustrates the power of publicity. It also recaps many of the same ideas that are in the release. It's important to utilize your cover letter. Remember, your release and cover letter can easily be separated. You don't want to lose out on a media opportunity, simply because an editor or producer has misplaced your release.

One Size Doesn't Fit All

Don't rely solely on one press release to do all of your work. Seldom do you have to write a completely new release, but you should modify the release to reflect the needs of the media outlet you're sending it to. Your release may just need a few minor changes. For example, let's say you are sending your release to your local evening news and to a parenting magazine. The main body of the release may not change, but you will want to modify some of the text before sending it to the editor at *Parenting* magazine, to reflect why your story will be of interest to his or her readers.

You need to realize who the audience is and direct your pitch towards the needs of that audience. Keep your releases simple, direct, and to the point. Just give enough information to pique their interest. For example, if you are a psychotherapist who has written a new book on how to make a relationship last, you don't want your press release to explain exactly what the book is about, you want to list the problems your book will help solve and the questions it helps couples answer. Emphasize that you offer solutions to specific relationship-oriented problems. Your job is to establish yourself as an expert, as a problem solver. The media isn't interested in hyping your book, they're interested in stories that interest their readers, listeners, or viewers. If you simply state that yours is the best book in the field, no one will care. Make the release as easy to read as possible, keep a lot of white space on the page, bullets, boxes, anything to break up the page. Remember this is a trailer, a tease. Give the media a story.

Chapter Seven

*The Release is Done—
Now What?*

7

THE RELEASE IS DONE—
NOW WHAT?

Now that the press release is ready to go—it's time to let it do its work. Do you know the right contact to send the release to? Are you sending it to the right address, fax, or e-mail? If you are sending a business-oriented press release to a magazine, you don't want to send it to the beauty editor. Do your homework. Study the masthead, which is located in the front of every magazine and lists who the various editors are and what sections they edit. Or better yet, call the magazine and ask whom you should address the release to. There are companies that sell media information, but often it's worth taking some time and making phone calls. Editors and segment producers are constantly changing; it's a business in continual flux, and if you buy a list or get a book that tells you who the editors or segment producers are, chances are that it will be out-of-date before you receive it.

You don't have to approach all of the media at once. Come up with a select list that you want to approach, a list of your initial target media. You may want to start off approaching no more than ten or fifteen media outlets. If you are faxing, check to make sure you have the correct number. If you are mailing, confirm the address. Also, invest a few dollars in stationery. After all that work, you want it to look as good as it reads, as it goes out the door.

A' Faxing We Will Go

If you are faxing your releases, make sure to fax them out with a cover sheet that clearly lists the specific person you are contacting. As I previously mentioned, the cover letter is more than just an address page; use it to restate much of the same information you have in the press release, but in an even more concise form. Try to edit it down to one or two short paragraphs. Only give the skeleton of the story, repeating the same ideas but wording them differently. I suggest you do this because faxes are often lost or misplaced, and the editor or producer ends up with only your cover sheet. If so, all is not lost—he or she still has the important information. Once again, the cover letter is never to exceed one page. Make sure your cover sheet includes your name and number. If you are announcing an event, or your release is time-specific, make sure to list the time, date, and address on the cover sheet. Remember, if the media wants more information, you can always give it to them later.

Welcome To The Minefield

We have now arrived at the minefield—to follow-up or not to follow-up. The media is not overly fond of follow-up calls. They get hundreds of calls a day and most are from people who are trying to convince them to do a story. Put yourself in the place of an editor or segment producer. You have a story to finish. You're on deadline and every five minutes you're receiving calls from people trying to sell you another inappropriate story idea, or trying to monopolize your time. After a while you get angry, and rightfully so.

If you are unprofessional, or harass the media, you're going to destroy any interest that your release may have created. I suggest waiting at least one week after sending out a release before even considering making calls. If you do call, remember, *you are calling to make sure that they received the information. You are not calling to beg or cajole them to do a story.*

But I'm A Natural Salesman—They Love Me

You may be a natural salesman, and your clients may indeed love you, but you're playing a different game here. You are entering a very specific phone world. You may be a great person one-on-one, with a winning smile and a firm handshake, but that won't get you far over the phone. You may be an extremely successful high-pressure tele-marketer, but remember, here you're dealing with a different, more weary, more sophisticated audience. Making follow-up calls can be a difficult proposition. Be candid with yourself. Do you have a person-ality that works over the phone? *If the phone intimidates you, or if you come off gruff, demanding, or impatient over the phone, don't make the calls, hire someone to make them on your behalf.*

You need to be painfully honest with yourself. Most of us don't like to admit that there are areas that aren't our forte. But none of us are proficient in everything. I don't particularly like phone conversations. But it took me some time to come to terms with the fact that I should-n't be doing the follow-up work. I felt guilty. I should do it, like it, and be effective. I was wrong. My strengths lie in developing campaign overviews and strategies, creating hooks and story ideas, writing releases, letters, bios, and in-person meetings. When it comes to my strengths and talents, making follow-up calls is not on my short list.

It took me some time, but I finally figured it out. I hired Steve Allen (no, not that Steve Allen) who does place phone work on his short list. Steve has made an art out of phone work. As the company grew, I hired others who possessed the gift of follow-ups. Now by blending my strengths with theirs we have created an extremely ef-fective and successful media placement company.

Don't try to be everything to all people. If you're uncomfortable on the phone, too demanding, or too pushy, you're only going to hurt your chances for success. You may be a good general in your business, but what you need here is a diplomat. You may not even be aware that you have a weak phone voice, or you're too aggressive, or your tone is too confrontational over the phone. Stand back and evaluate yourself objectively. Ask someone whom you trust to give you feedback. It will do you no good to alienate the media by making poor follow-up calls. All you'll end up doing is ruining your campaign.

The Ol' "I'll Hold My Breath Until You Print My Story" Approach

It's surprising how many people approach the media in a confrontational or threatening way—almost berating the media if they pass on a story idea. Remember editors and segment producers have thousands upon thousands of stories pitched to them every day. *They don't need your story, they need a story that fits their audience. Your job is to make your story one that meets their needs.* So don't demand they use your ideas. Don't try to bully the media or beat them into submission. Become a resource. Keep developing story ideas. These are people whom you want as your allies.

Follow-Up Suicide

I have tried to position my firm as a resource instead of a sales force. Go in with a bullying, used-car salesman approach and you've already lost the battle. *They don't need you.* If you push them, they will make that absolutely clear to you. Media placement has nothing to do with fairness. I knew one person who used to call up editors and producers and angrily give them a piece of his mind whenever they ran a story on his competitors' product. The sad part was that his product was superior to that of his rival, but, because of how he dealt with the media, he was avoided like the plague. *No one wanted to do a story on his product, because no one wanted to do a story on him.* Don't waste your time trying to convince the media why you are right or trying to make a hard sale. Your objective is to meet their needs and, in turn, meet yours. You are working to build a professional relationship.

The Follow-Up Etiquette

If you are going to make follow-up calls, initially concentrate on your local media. The local press will usually be more open to your calls and pitches. Keep your calls brief (five minutes maximum) and be polite. Be up and enthusiastic. Don't spend your time explaining why yours is the best store or product in town, or why they will be missing the story of the century if they don't use your idea—everyone tells them that. Never beg or berate the media. You're calling to introduce yourself. Make sure they have the information, and ask if they need any other corroborating information. Don't be pushy, but be assertive. Don't sound intimidating. Be up and polite. Listen to the editor's or producer's feedback. If the person on the other line can't talk, acts harried, or says no, remember, chances are you caught him or her right in the middle of a story deadline. Don't push it. Politely say thank you and hang up.

If the person on the other line starts a dialogue or asks you questions, be open, keep the conversation going, but don't try to do a sales job. *You are not there to sell anything, but to be a resource.* If you're told there's no interest in your story, don't try to bulldoze them. Find out if there are any stories they are currently working on that you could help out with. Find out what kind of stories that particular editor or segment producer usually works on.

Your initial follow-up call is to make sure that your information arrived and was seen by the right person, and to introduce yourself. Keep the call short, polite, and very much to the point. Be courteous and quickly get off the phone. Although it is almost impossible to be effective by simply sending out press releases or media information, be prudent in the calls you make. Don't call until you have given your release a chance to do its job. Without follow-up calls, media placement is often a real crapshoot, yet the wrong kind of follow-up calls will knock you out of the game completely. Nine times out of ten, you will call only to find out that no one saw your fax or received your letter. If that is the case, during the conversation, give a quick thumbnail sketch of your release, and ask if you can re-send it, and thank them for their time. Be polite and get off quickly. And don't call back twenty minutes later to see if they are now free to talk. Be judicious in your calls. In time you will cultivate a working relationship with some of the media and begin to develop your own, unique follow-up etiquette. Until then, my advice is to err on the side of prudence.

Chapter Eight

More Media to Keep in Mind

8

MORE MEDIA TO KEEP IN MIND

Although we've covered the basics, the following is a quick overview
of potential media outlets, as well as a review of media time lines to
keep in mind before sending out information.

Television

Remember to target your local media, including cable and community college TV. Keep in mind that community-oriented early morning
news programs and morning talk shows will often focus on one specific topic. Study the last ten minutes of broadcast on the local news.
That time slot usually features lighter news, human interest, or new
product-oriented stories that you can fit into.

When pitching national talk shows think in terms of themes. Don't
just pitch information on yourself, but explain how you and your story
can fit the particular show's format.

Never forget that TV is visual. Try to offer the producer more than
just a talking head. Are there any interesting visuals you can offer? Is
your product, store, or office visually interesting? Think visually.

TV Time Line

When sending press releases or information to television programs, always send your information three days to one week in advance. If you are approaching national shows, or the TV talk shows, allow two to four weeks.

Magazines

Study the various publication's demographics and pitch your stories accordingly. Think in terms of trends when pitching stories to such publications as *Time* or *Newsweek*. Don't limit yourself to the well-known publications. Keep magazine guides in mind as potential media outlets. These guides are usually distributed in hotels and in some restaurants. Also look for special-interest publications in your field. These are magazines that are devoted to one particular field or area.

Magazine Time Line

When pitching a story to a weekly magazine, send your information one month to six weeks in advance. If pitching a monthly magazine, make sure to get your information to the editor a minimum of three months in advance.

Newspapers

Never overlook club newsletters, church bulletins, business association newsletters, and small publications. For the local press, develop a local hook that is community-oriented. Although there have been countless stories predicting the death of newspapers, remember, over one-half of the country receives a daily paper. This is an extremely powerful, multi-billion dollar industry. Offer to write articles for trade, community-based, or local publications, free of charge. Also keep in mind ethnic papers, which are rapidly growing around the country.

Newspaper Time Line

If you are pitching a daily or metro newspaper, make sure to allow a minimum of two weeks. When pitching a weekly or biweekly paper, allow a minimum of three weeks.

Radio

As of 1994, there were a total of 11,556 radio stations in the U.S. Pitch the nationally syndicated talk shows, as well as your local radio shows, but if you have a book or a product to sell, don't neglect the various regional radio talk shows.

Radio Time Line

Pitch a story to a radio program at least two weeks in advance.

Newswire Services

Newswire services such as AP, UPI, and Reuters gather information and provide stories to other media. The stories are written by the service's reporters and transmitted to newsrooms around the country. Newswire services also have a daybook, which lists the day's newsworthy events. Remember, wire services feed the regional and the national press. Work on developing stories that have a national or a broad regional appeal.

Newswire Time Line

When pitching a story to a wire service, make sure to send your information a minimum of two weeks in advance.

Also keep in mind that there are other forms of marketing that you can utilize to help your company or career grow, including newsletters, special events, seminars and workshops, trade shows, speeches, lectures, and networking. They can all be effective, but are best utilized in conjunction with an effective media placement campaign. None can offer you the exposure of one well-placed story.

Chapter Nine

The T.V. Crew is On Its Way

9

THE TV CREW IS ON ITS WAY

You sent out your release, pitched your story, and a TV producer liked it. Either she/he called you, or when you made your follow-up call you were told that the story sounded interesting, and were asked to send more information.

The Myth of the Press Kit

More information? You don't have more information. What other information should you send? This is one of those times when you can utilize a press kit. What's a press kit, you ask? Good question. A press kit generally consists of a two-pocket folder in which you include your press release, fact sheet, and a biography on yourself and your company. You can also include a photo, some graphics, statistics, visuals, a brochure, a sample list of questions, and a Rolodex card. Some companies include buttons, audio tapes, video tapes, booklets, whistles, trinkets, knickknacks, you name it and someone has jammed it into a press kit. There are companies that spend hundreds of thousands of dollars on extravagant, expensive press kits. Trouble is, most press kits get tossed in the circular file as soon as they arrive at the editor's or producer's desk. Most don't make it past the secretary. A press kit's travel itinerary generally goes something like this—your office, post office, media outlet office, trash can.

Press kits can cost thousands of dollars, which can translate into a hefty profit for many public relations companies. I'm sure that I'll be at odds with other public relations professionals, but I generally find press kits to be a waste of time and money. They're expensive and usually don't do the job they're intended to do. I've found that press kits are generally ego-oriented. People want to make a splash. They want to look good. They want to keep up with the competition. Often the head of a company will see a competitor's press kit and immediately demand that his graphics department design one that's glossier, snazzier, and thicker. But the bottom line is, why do you want a press kit? Press kits can be invaluable when making presentations to clients, or for internal public relations, but think twice before sending them to the media. And never send a press kit out as your first contact. If the media requests a press kit, by all means send one. That's when they should be used. But don't send out a hundred press kits at random, and never send a press kit to inappropriate media.

Speaker's Press Kit

While we're on the topic of press kits, don't confuse a speaker's press kit with a publicity press kit. A speaker's press kit is used to help professionals in various fields land speaking engagements. They differ from publicity press kits and should never be sent to the media. A speaker's press kit traditionally includes a brochure, topic of speech offered, title and speech outline, copies of testimonials, list of clients the speaker has addressed, a list of services offered, fee schedule, tear sheets, bio, black-and-white photo, cover letter, and a copy of the contract.

Know What You're Sending, When To Send It, And To Whom You're Sending It

When I worked as an editor, I would receive several press kits a day. But I seldom if ever really looked at them. I never had the time. I had a magazine to edit, and press kits were filled with too much self-serving information to be of interest. There was too much information to digest, too many pages to read, and nine times out of ten it was all fluff. All of the glossy folders, colored paper, photos, buttons, and other paraphernalia did me no good. I was looking for a story, not a self-serving carnival. A one-paragraph story idea was infinitely more valuable to me than any expensive, extravagant press kit.

Once I was meeting with an editor at *Cosmopolitan* Magazine and we happened to hit upon the topic of press kits. She leaned over and pulled two huge press kits out of the trash can by the side of her desk and handed them to me. Both were kits featuring off-road races that had been sent to her by car companies. Mind you, these kits were not sent to the advertising department, but to the editorial department of *Cosmopolitan*. "Why would they send me these," she complained. "It just wastes my time. It shows they have no idea what our magazine is about, and they don't care to take the time to find out." She then smiled, took them back, and returned them to the trash can. *The moral is, know what you're sending, when to send it, and whom to send it to.* Be judicious when sending out kits, have a couple of basic kits available in case the media requests one, but don't send them out at random. And never, ever send out a kit without sending along some story ideas. Don't make the media do your work for you.

The only reason to send a press kit is to give an editor or producer more pertinent information on you and your company, and *pertinent* is the operative word here. Unless you have a very green reporter who is influenced by a lot of flash and glitter, all of that gloss and colored paper isn't going to matter a bit. If you are asked to send more information, first ask if you can answer any questions over the phone. We've often been able to answer the media's questions and schedule an interview or story without having to send further information. Be prepared, anticipate any questions the media will ask, and have all of your answers and information ready.

But let's say that the media still wants to see more information. Fine. Have a basic kit ready. Include a biography on yourself, a fact sheet on your company or business, which can include information that you want to highlight, copies of any media you have appeared in, and a cover letter addressing any questions that you think should be answered. You may want to include a photo, visuals, anecdotal stories that illustrate why your story is interesting, and some statistics. Keep it simple and keep it concise. Information is what you want to give them, not flash and glitter.

You're Ready, Right?

Okay, you've put together your press kit and mailed it out. Three days later the producer phones and informs you that the story is a go. She wants to shoot the segment at 8:30 tomorrow morning, and she'll have a crew at your store at that time. Great. It worked. You've done it. Only, what do you do now?

Media Training

Have you practiced conducting mock interviews? Have you done some media training, even if it's only with a friend? Media training is—surprise—training to appear on the media. There are companies that specialize in media training. They teach their clients how to dress, what to say, and the type of body language to use.

Ann Convery, M.A., who specializes in media training and communications, conducts the media training for my company. She coaches clients on how to present themselves and their message. Her sessions, which I have to admit are the best available, are videotaped, which allows clients to take the tapes home, review the information, and study their presentation. She is a pro and can guide a client through the possible mine fields, preparing them for interviews with anyone from Bill Moyers to Howard Stern. In addition to being my personal media trainer, she is also my wife. The following are some of her training tips.

Media Training Tips

1. Practice projecting: Pretend you're at a dinner party and you are entertaining the entire table with what you do. This is you at your best: pithy, funny, warm, passionate about your job. This is the same you that should appear in front of the camera.

2. Remember those three main points that you want to get across. Practice working one of your three most important points into each answer that you give.

3. Don't rely on "unhearable" words to describe your product. We all use them. Words like safe, effective, fantastic, good, nice, great and perfect. The problem is that we overuse them and they become meaningless.

4. Tell a short, funny story about your product that makes it new and fresh.

5. Radio and especially TV are time sensitive mediums. You may have two or three minutes to answer questions. Don't ramble! Make your answers a minute or less. Tell your stories in two minutes or less.

6. Don't drop the ball. There is nothing worse than a one or two word answer followed by dead air. If the answer to a question you are asked is yes, don't simply say yes and stare at the interviewer waiting for the next question to be asked. That's not only dull and non-informative, it's rude. You aren't holding your end of the conversation up. Help the interviewer out. This isn't an exam. Answer in such a way that you provoke another question. Think dialogue.

7. If they mispronounce your name, smile and correct them, nicely!

8. If they don't mention your location, work this into your answers.

9. Take control of the interview. If you sense that they are not asking you the "right" questions, that's fine. You are going to work the three key points of your message into your answers anyway, and you will both be satisfied.

10. Don't hide behind your information. Some people feel that what is interesting about them is their information, and they rattle off the answers obediently. You are there to connect first, then inform. People connect with people, not facts.

Once you've reached this point, even if you have hired a public relations firm to handle your campaign, you and you alone have to take over. How you look, how you sound, your demeanor—these are now what become important. Studies show that 93 percent of what an audience reacts to has to do with the messenger, and only 7 percent has to do with the message itself. Remember, you are the messenger and the messenger must sell the message.

Hey, I'm No Actor!

You don't have to be an actor, you just have to be professional, and that takes practice. I suggest everyone take at least a few hours of professional media training, especially before appearing on television. But, even if you choose not to hire a professional, you have to do some training before being interviewed by the media.

Make yourself a basic check list. Do you have a list of the main points you want to cover? Have you stood in front of a mirror and asked yourself some anticipated questions, reviewing how you'll answer them and how you'll look? Have you asked a co-worker or friend to conduct a mock interview with you? Have you reviewed your wardrobe, your outer image? No? Well, time's wasting, you only have a few hours before all of your work can start to pay off. You owe it to yourself to give the media the best presentation and interview you can. But, as you can see, and hear from the knocking of your knees, you haven't finished your work, you've just started.

All of these issues should obviously be addressed before you send out your first press release. But most people don't prepare themselves. There have been several times when this has happened to us. We sign a client, and an hour later the media calls looking for an expert and the new client perfectly fits the bill. What do we do? Each situation is different.

We recently signed a client who was launching a new cosmetic line primarily targeted to Latinas. The very day we signed her, we received a call from a producer at *NBC* News who was putting together a piece on cosmetics and wanted to interview an expert. We also received a call from a producer at a major talk show that was putting together a show on beauty and was looking for a company that specialized in cosmetics for minorities. The *NBC* spot shot the following day. There was no time for media training, in this case. But, because the client, although somewhat nervous, was a good spokesperson and could handle the interview, we scheduled it. There have been other times when we have had to reschedule, or even lose an interview, because the client was simply not prepared.

Prepare, Prepare, Prepare

Because our company is known to the media as a resource, we continually receive calls from print and electronic media looking for story ideas. Although media placement usually takes some time, there are those instances when a press release immediately hits the jackpot. We have faxed out a press release on a client at 9 a.m. and have had that client doing a live TV interview at noon that same day. You have to be ready. Remember, don't unleash the magic of the media until you're prepared to control it. Be patient. Make sure you have everything in order before you start. Once it's in motion, it's too late. And, if you're not prepared to do the interview, it could turn out to be a dismal experience. You'll feel depressed and embarrassed, the media will feel cheated, and you will have wasted an incredible opportunity.

So prepare. Review the image you want to convey: small town and friendly, authoritative, professional, humorous, avant-garde, formal and business-like—whatever. But make sure that your image matches your personality. If you are basically shy and retiring, don't try to come off like a rock star. It ain't gonna work. You may have to learn to project more and become a bit more forceful with your responses, but those are simply tools you learn to utilize when needed. Keep your voice modulated. Be dynamic, but not frenzied. Your mission here is not to alter your personality, but to enhance it.

It's The Look

Review your wardrobe. You don't want to wear white, stripes, checks, or geometric designs that will drive the viewers crazy. Find what colors look best on you. Wear something attractive, but something you're comfortable in. Don't wear clothes that are too tight because you think they make you look thinner. Wear clothes that reflect who you are and the work you do. Remember, when dealing with the visual media, your image and presentation has a greater impact on people than what you say.

Sit in front of a mirror and practice your body language. Sit erect, but try not to look stiff. Find someone to play the role of the interviewer and do a couple of mock interviews. Practice eye contact. Speak clearly and succinctly. Establish rapport with the interviewer. Choose two or three main points and practice getting them across within the context of the questions asked. Don't ramble. Don't take two paragraphs to answer a question that you could answer in two sentences. Be clear and specific. Practice taking control of the situation. Remember your message.

Let's say you're an attorney located in the Silicon Valley area, and you're being interviewed on the local news. You specialize in working with small businesses, specifically software companies, and want small business owners to view you as a specialist in the field. So what are the three main points you want to get across? To start with, you want prospective clients to know where you're located, you want them to know the type of work you do, and you want them to view you as *the* person to call for their business needs.

You are being interviewed about how new changes in the tax laws will affect small businesses. You want to meet the media's needs as well as your own. In my experience, the best way to cover all of the bases is by telling an anecdotal story. If the interviewer asks you what impact the new tax laws are having, be prepared to answer the question by telling a story. For example, "Because I'm based in the heart of Silicon Valley, and work with quite a few software companies, I've seen the effect that the new tax laws have on businesses first-hand." By framing your reply this way you have achieved two objectives: the viewers now know where you're located and they know your expertise. Your two primary objectives have been met. You can now relax and continue the interview. If you can get a few more points in, great, but if not, you've already accomplished your objectives.

It sounds like a lot, but if you practice, once the interview starts, you will be prepared and effective. And after the first few interviews, this will all become second nature to you. It's not unlike driving a car. If I were to list all of the steps involved in getting into the car, putting on the seat belt, starting the ignition, etc., it would be a long list. To someone who had never driven before, it would seem daunting, but once you do it a few times it becomes automatic. You don't have to think about it, you just do it.

Talking In Media Morse Code

Keep in mind the communication power of sound bytes. Sound bites are quick, colorful, easy-to-understand responses. No one really talks in sound bites, at least no one you'd want to be around for any amount of time, which is why you need to practice. Think of sound bites as a type of entertaining Morse Code. You have no time for the superficial, you only want to get across the essential information, but you want to do it in an interesting way. You might be interviewed for half an hour but only end up with two minutes of air time. So work on developing a few short sentences that are fun and help get your message across. Although they can be witty, cute, or clever, you don't want to go over-board and become too precious.

Sound Bite Examples:

Herbologist: "Antibiotics are actually quite new to health care. Herbs have been used medicinally for thousands of years, yet we call herbs alternative. Herbs allow your body to heal naturally. I want the American public to reach in their medicine cabinet and find a bottle of herbs next to the bottle of aspirin.

Optician: "The right pair of eyeware is like an inexpensive facelift! Instead of heading for the plastic surgeon, just get the right pair of frames. Your face will look lifted and leaner."

Accountant: "I not only take care of my client's accounting, I work with my clients to demystify the process. I make certain the IRS won't make my client's lives a mess."

Clothing Designer: "My aim is not to sell a piece of clothing, but to instill a sense of style. If I sell a woman an outfit, she will look good for a while, but if I can give her a sense of her own, unique style, she will look good for the rest of her life. It's not about the label, it's about you."

Now that I think about it, that clothing designer is on the right track. What you want to do is develop your own innate sense of style in your delivery and presentation. It may take some time to find sound bites that seem to fit. Play with them. Eventually you'll find the right ones. Keep in mind that you want a couple of sound bites that you can pepper into the conversation, but you definitely do not want your entire conversation to be a series of sound bites. Some people become obsessed with finding clever ways to turn a phrase. Sound bites are just an aid. Find a couple that you can use, and move on.

The media is not only looking for content, but for someone who can deliver the content or information in an interesting manner. Once the interview starts, you'll only have a short period of time to present your message, and most of what you say will end up on the cutting room floor, so be concise, practice, and cut away the verbal fat.

I can't overemphasize the power of effective anecdotal stories. For example, if you're a dermatologist located in Los Angeles, I'd suggest mentioning that since you're located in L.A. where the sun is out 12 months a year, you do a lot of skin cancer screening. Anything that ties your profession to your location—that's how people will find you. If you are on a national show and no one mentions what state or city you're in, you're in trouble.

Good. You've done your homework. You've worked on talking in sound bites and presenting your message in an entertaining, clear, and concise manner. Now, take some deep breaths, close your eyes, and center yourself—relax. What you are striving for is a relaxed and natural presentation. Think of the last time that you were truly excited about something, or the last time you were telling a friend about a wonderful experience or exhilarating trip you took. That is the energy and excitement that you want to recapture when talking to the media. Now, what if you only had three minutes to convey everything you wanted to say? What would you keep? What would you cut? What words would you use? Simply talking more rapidly wouldn't help; you'd sound rushed, not enthusiastic. No, you'd try to edit your story. You'd be specific, hit the high points. You'd talk in sound bytes.

You can have energy and enthusiasm, without turning into Phyllis

Diller or Richard Simmons. Your objective is to present your information in layman's terms, without using technical or inside jargon. You want to get the information across as concisely and succinctly as possible, with no rambling or digressing. And you want to entertain your audience. Always keep your audience in mind. You don't need or want to be theatrical or comedic. What you want to be is compelling. Do your homework, define your message, and be yourself—you'll be successful.

Chapter Ten

Whatdaya Mean,
Pre-Interview?

10

WHATDAYA MEAN, PRE-INTERVIEW?

Now let's take a common scenario. An associate producer from a local TV program called you. He is interested in having you appear on the show, but before scheduling an appearance, he would like to schedule a phone pre-interview with a senior producer. Pre-interview? What's a pre-interview?

First of all, congratulations. You've won round one. What it means is that the producer likes your information and is interested in having you appear on the program, but before having you on, he wants to make sure that you can deliver the goods. Will you make a good guest for the program? Are you a good interview? That is going to be determined by how well you do on the phone pre-interview. I can't emphasize strongly enough how important pre-interviews are. If you take them lightly and decide not to practice or prepare your information, chances are you're going to fail to impress the producer, and you'll never make it as a guest on the show. I've had clients lose national shows because they refused to prepare for the pre-interview. They figured that they'd dazzle them once they got on the show. It's like a comedian saving his best material for the *Tonight Show*. Well, if no one sees how funny he is, he's never going to get on the *Tonight Show*. The pre-interview is of vital importance. Often it's more difficult than the actual interview itself. Remember, there are droves of people trying to get on that very program that's interested in you. If you don't deliver the goods, someone else will. So be prepared.

What's It All About?

Make sure you understand exactly what the interview is about and what the media wants from you. Don't be shy. Ask questions. Make sure you understand exactly what the producer is looking for. The initial objective is to meet that particular story's needs. Once you've accomplished that, you can work on meeting your own needs. Find out exactly what they're looking for, so you can clearly discuss the topic. Find out if you are going to be the lone guest, if it's going to be a panel, or if there is going to be a guest representing an opposing view. Find out as much as you can. If you have any facts or information that will help the segment, let the producer know, but don't just give him a litany of fact after fact. If necessary, during the pre-interview, have your information written out in front of you, but only use it as a reference. Keep in mind you won't have this luxury on the show itself.

If you're an insurance salesperson, you may want to talk about a special type of policy you offer, but the media may only want to talk about the national trends in the insurance business. *Give them what they want.* Do your homework. Have statistics and examples at your fingertips. You may be able to use your new policy as an example of a trend, but don't try to change the scope of the interview. If the producer feels that all you want to do is turn the segment into a commercial for your business, he is going to thank you for your time and find another insurance expert to appear on the program.

Once you understand what the segment is about and do some homework... can you tie in an event or topic that is currently in the news? Work on developing story ideas that revolve around the news, current events, and topical issues. Study the media. You can help make it a bigger story by tying into a story that has some national prominence. Don't get bogged down here. This isn't essential, but it can help. For example, we were once working with a cosmetic surgeon who specialized in male-oriented procedures. Around that time, President Clinton had been in the news for having delayed his plane's take-off in order to get a haircut. We came up with a campaign entitled "The New Male Vanity" and used this news incident to illustrate the point that men, starting with the President, were becoming more and more interested in their appearance. This not only caught the media's attention, it also gave producers and editors a piece of information to lead off the story.

Sample Questions

Make a list of a minimum of 15 optimum questions that can be passed on to the media. These questions should be designed to give the producer a road map, an outline to work from, but they should also allow you to address and discuss the issues and topics that are of prime concern to you. Be sure to send them to the producer before the pre-interview.

Let's say that you're an interior designer. You specialize in helping your clients express their distinct personalities in their homes and work places. You have a strong background in design and offer one-on-one personalized service. You are also skilled at keeping the expenses down for clients who are working on a specific budget. The list of sample questions would read something like:

1. How did you start working in the field of interior design?
2. What about interior design interests you the most?
3. How long have you worked in the field?
4. How are you different from other designers?
5. Give us some examples of work you've done.
6. Does someone need a big budget to hire a designer?
7. Can you help your clients find custom-designed products?
8. Give us a step-by-step rundown of how the process works.
9. Does a person have to know exactly what they want before calling you?
10. What are the most common interior design mistakes?

11. What if your tastes differ from those of your clients?
12. How closely do you work with the client?
13. What are the smallest and largest spaces you've worked on?
14. How are your fees structured?
15. Are there some basic interior design rules to keep in mind?
16. How long does it usually take to design an office or work-place?

These are basic questions, but you are helping to shape the interview. Never list a question on your sheet until you know the answer. Sample questions help both the interviewer and the interviewee. They give you both a starting point. But, don't assume, because you have given the producer a list of questions, that those are the questions you'll be asked. There are interviewers who hate being fed questions. They know what they want to ask and they'll ask what they want. There are other times when your questions are tossed out for no apparent reason.

Not long ago, we had a client appear on a national TV show. Before the taping, the producer reviewed the questions that the interviewer would ask. The producer was very specific with my client, outlining the scope of the interview, as well as what questions would be asked and in what order. Well, once the interview actually began, none of the questions that had been discussed were asked. The questions that were asked weren't tough or controversial, they just weren't the questions that my client had been told would be asked. So, be prepared to answer your sample questions, but be even more prepared to be asked questions that aren't on your list. What it comes down to is *know your field*—and *Prepare*.

Different Strokes For Different Folks

Don't ever go on a program before you have seen it. Watch the program. Study it and modify your answers to suit the particular needs of that show. Remember, the needs of a TV talk show differ from those of a news program, daily newspaper, magazine, or radio program.

A TV evening news program needs to present all of the breaking news. Examples would be international turmoil, disasters, or fluctuations in the economy, you know—the mandatory stuff, the hard news. But news programs also run soft news stories. These are personal interest stories or profiles of unique businesses, individuals, or services. The soft news category is where your story will most likely fit. For example, in the soft news category, we have placed such stories as *Understanding the Internet*, *The Latest Skin Care Beauty Secrets*, *Nutritional Super Supplements*, *Fashion Tips For Men*, and *Holiday Exercise Tips*. We have also placed harder-edged stories on a new cancer breakthrough, a Congressional race, and a Presidential race. Although these were more serious in their scope, they were still not mandatory, hard news stories. We still had to work to place them in the media.

Talk shows are usually theme-driven. The whole program may revolve around one specific theme. *Oprah* and *Leeza* are examples of theme-driven shows. Others are divided into segments in which each segment is devoted to a specific topic, and others, such as *Regis & Kathie Lee*, are guest-driven. Guest-driven shows tend to be interested primarily in celebrities and, except in rare instances, will be a waste of your time. Each program and magazine and newspaper is different, so do your homework before pitching.

Remember, It's Entertainment

During the pre-interview, relax, listen, and answer the producer's questions. Don't anticipate questions before they are asked. Don't talk over the interviewer in an effort to give him your whole story. You are being interviewed here, but it's also a conversation—allow it to have a conversational flow. Establish rapport with the interviewer. If you don't know an answer to a specific question, be honest about it. But definitely let the interviewer know that you can find the answer. If you don't understand a question, ask the interviewer to ask it again.

Remember your main points. Keep the interview in perspective.

The bottom line is that even the news is entertainment, and although the producer wants to make sure you are an expert in your field, he also needs to feel confident that you can hold the viewers' interest. You are there to interest as well as inform the audience. You don't have to be an entertainer, just be up, energetic; keep it interesting.

Chapter Eleven

On To The Interview

11

ON TO THE INTERVIEW

Congratulations, you made it through the pre-interview, and the producer has booked you on the TV program. You have joined an elite group. This is what you've worked towards. Knock 'em dead.

You've reviewed your wardrobe and dressed appropriately. If you're discussing a product or a book, you've made sure that you're taking along some extra samples (you have already sent copies to the producer). You're about to walk out to your car, you've given yourself plenty of time (keep in mind—if you're late, you're dead), and you are ready to drive to the station and experience your first interview. Before you pull out of the driveway, be on the safe side, take a couple of minutes (you've given yourself plenty of time, right?) and review the following checklist.

Interview Check List

1. Review the two or three primary facts that you want to get across during the interview.
2. Make sure you've checked yourself in a mirror before you go on camera. Is your hair in place? Is your tie crooked? Is your lipstick smeared? Give yourself the basic once-over.

3. Once the interview begins, remember, you don't have to force the information; weave your points into the interview. If you spend your time forcing an issue, it will come out sounding strained and stilted.

4. Relax. You are there to have a conversation. Well, at least you want it to look like a conversation.

5. No slouching. Sit erect.

6. Focus on the interviewer. The camera and crew is part of the furniture as far as you're concerned.

7. Start off with your most important information. Interviews can be very short. If you don't lead with what's important, you may have missed your chance.

8. Breathe. People have a tendency to hold their breath when nervous, which only creates more anxiety. Remember to breathe.

9. Smile. I've seen more media opportunities ruined by people who have refused to smile during their interviews. Looking grave does not make you appear more profound, it makes you look dull and somber.

10. Listen. Don't anticipate questions. Don't think that you know what the interviewer is asking. Wait until the question is asked and then respond.

11. If you get momentarily confused, or lose your train of thought, that's okay. It happens to everyone. Take a deep breath and start again.

12. It's all right to ask the interviewer to repeat a question. The last thing you want to do is give an answer to a question you don't fully understand.

13. If the interviewer takes the conversation into an area you're not comfortable with, or tries to manipulate you into answering questions that you don't want to answer, remember you have control over the situation. Don't be forced into saying something you don't want to say. Be polite, but say what you want to say.

14. If a particular question throws you, or if you don't want to answer a specific question, deflect it. Acknowledge that it was asked, and then return to an area that you're comfortable addressing. You see and hear these types of responses every day around election time. An example of an appropriate response would be: "I certainly understand why you'd ask that question, but what's really important is...," now return to your agenda.

15. If you have three main points that you want to make and you are only able to mention one of them, don't worry. You'll get 'em next time.

16. Don't recite a laundry list of information and sacrifice a good interview. We've all had teachers who knew their subjects well, but bored the hell out of us. That may work in school, because there's a captive audience, but you have no such luxury. You are there to interest as well as inform the audience.

17. Don't be vague or use trade jargon. Speak in easy-to-understand language.

18. Show the audience what you're talking about. Use a story or an account that illustrates a point, as opposed to just giving them vague ideas or theories.

19. Keep your information concise, and to the point. Keep it clear and easy to understand.

20. When trying to make a particular point, be assertive but not pushy.

21. Mention your location. Although interviewers will often give your exact address over the air, many won't. That's why, if one of your objectives is to attract clients or patients, always mention where your practice or business is located. You don't need to give the exact address. That will sound like a commercial. But you can make sure that the audience knows the general area where you're located. This may not be a huge concern if you're appearing on a local TV program in a small town, but it becomes very important if you are being interviewed on a national show, or if you live in a large metropolis like Los Angeles or New York. The viewers may love you, but if they

can't find you, you're in trouble. For example, if you own a health spa in the Palm Springs area, you can explain that, because your spa is located in Palm Springs, you have developed special treatments and products to combat the effects that the dry, desert heat can have on skin. Make your location a part of your story. Don't simply blurt out your address, but weave your location into the conversation.

22. Relax. Have fun. You've worked hard for this—enjoy it.

The Many Faces Of An Interview

Interviews take many forms. A TV interview can be held at a studio, at your place of business, or at an event. I have had clients interviewed in studios, offices, laboratories, parks, operating rooms, political rallies, cars, parking lots, factories, conventions, street corners—you name it. One day you can be sitting on an elaborate set, with multiple cameras and a studio audience, and the next day end up in an empty room talking into a portable camera, where the interviewer, camera person and sound person are all one and the same.

Magazine and newspaper interviews often take place over the phone. Although, in the case of a feature story, chances are you will have an in-person interview with the reporter. Some reporters write notes, some use tape recorders, and still others seem to record everything in their brain (although I have no idea how they accomplish this feat).

Radio interviews can be handled over the phone or in a studio, depending on the program and the situation. There are so many radio interview programs around the country that we often have clients doing several phone interviews in one day.

But whatever the media, and however and wherever the interview takes place, your basic objectives remain the same. Stay centered and remember your message. The more interviews you experience, the better you'll become at them, but don't ever go on automatic. Don't assume that you no longer have to prepare. Keep your checklist with you. The best athletes prepare for every game. Follow suit. Do your homework. Prepare for every interview.

Congratulations—But You've Only Just Begun

So, you've done it. You did your groundwork, put together a campaign, interested the media, and appeared on TV. You were a success. You received several phone calls after your appearance from prospective clients. Your business is growing. A newspaper editor saw the piece and is assigning a writer to interview you next week. It worked!

That was easy. It's all downhill from this point. You're happy, and now you can forget this publicity stuff and move on with your life. Dream on. You've just taken your first baby step, you're nowhere near walking. Forget about running. Remember media placement is a cumulative process. You have your first media interview under your belt now. You now have tape on yourself. You can change your release and bio to include that you were featured on the program. You are now, as they say in the film biz, a player. You're a rookie, but a player none the less. The first step is a huge step, but keep in mind it's still just the first step.

It is often at this point, after one or two interviews, that people tend to get cocky and forget the big picture. Keep your ego in check and remember your primary objectives. Have them in writing, so you can refer to them when you start to get off-track. Stay focused. Be patient, persistent, and realistic. Speaking of being realistic, it's time to shatter some of the most common and harmful PR myths.

Chapter Twelve

The Greatest PR Myths Of All Time

12

THE GREATEST PR MYTHS OF ALL TIME

Now that you have experienced some success and have a basic sense of the inner workings of publicity, chances are you're about to fall prey to one or more PR myths. You see, a little knowledge can be a dangerous thing. Because you understand some of the basics of publicity, don't assume you are now a PR Ph.D. People tend to overlook the fact that this is a subtle business. In publicity, often what appears to be the obvious decision is the wrong decision. What makes it especially difficult is that everyone thinks that they know all there is to know about publicity. You will be given advice from your neighbors, co-workers, pastors, janitors, clients, patients, relatives—you name it.

I once worked for a publisher who had a tendency to listen to, and take advice from, any and everyone he met. When he went to lunch, I used to pray that the elevator would be empty and that he'd go for drive-through fast food where no one would talk to him. If he spoke to a waitress, a salesperson, or a stranger in an elevator, he would invariably call me into his office and propose that we implement some revolutionary suggestions that he had been given. Never mind that nine times out of ten these changes were totally inappropriate, as far as he was concerned they were dynamic, new—revolutionary!

People love to give advice, whether they know what they're talking about or not. Remember, these people who tell you exactly how you should run your business have nothing at stake, which is why they can afford to make such definitive and authoritative pronouncements. So, when these know-it-alls give you advice, smile, listen, maybe even nod, but stay on course.

God knows there are more PR myths than I'm presenting here, but the following is a list of the most common mistakes I watch people make, day after day, after day, after....

I Can't Use National Media

We live in the information age. If you're resourceful and inventive enough, you can come up with an interesting story, hook, or idea that will interest the national media. I know, you think you could never garner national media—your story's simply not exciting enough. But you're wrong, *you can interest the national media.* No, you're probably thinking, even if you could land some national stories, you have no possible use for national media, so what difference does it make? It would just be a waste of time and money for you. You're based in a little town called Nowhereville, USA, so what good would a story that hits all fifty states do you? It's obvious I just don't understand your needs.

Well, let's see. As to your first point, that you don't have a story that could interest the national media: why not? Why couldn't you generate national interest in your story? Remember everyone who is quoted in *Time* magazine, or interviewed on the *Today* show lives and works in some local town or city. Take a look at all of the possible angles available. What makes your story different, unique? Is there some trend or new breakthrough in your field that affects not only your particular business, but your profession as a whole? Are there other similar types of businesses or professions that you can help weave into your story to give it a broader appeal? Study all the possibilities. Give your story a wider, more national scope.

For example, we have represented quite a few practitioners in the field of alternative health care, including herbologists, naturopaths, homeopaths, bodyworkers, and acupuncturists. There are alternative health care specialists spread out around the country, so why did

CNN, Vogue, Esquire, Today, Newsweek, NBC, The Los Angeles Times, and other national, regional, and local media decide to feature our clients?

Because we developed a series of story ideas and pitched them to the national media. We came up with overview stories on how alternative health care is impacting the country's health care system, statistics illustrating how many people are using alternative health care, the amount of dollars that are being spent on alternative health care, and how it is impacting our overall health care system. We developed an overview pitch that included various forms of alternative health care, including homeopathy, bodywork, and chiropractic work. We offered the media as many ideas as possible. We offered them stories based on various ways that alternative health care impacts our nation. Our pitch was not client-oriented, but story-oriented. We centered our pitch around the impact that alternative health care was having on the country. Our clients were presented as experts who could address the various issues. We did not pigeon-hole our clients as being locally-based practitioners, but as being representatives of a national trend. By pitching our clients as experts who could discuss a topic of national importance, we were able to transcend the local aspect.

Regardless of the field you are in, you want to pitch your story in a similar manner. By doing so, you remove the local or regional barrier. You are pitching a story that will interest the nation as a whole. Brainstorm, come up with different ideas. You'll find some, just give it time. Don't ignore your local angles. Use them for your local media, but remember, you can and should transcend your city boundary lines. From my experience, I've found that it's as easy, or as hard (depending on how you want to look at it), to place national media, as it is to land local and regional press.

Now let's look at why you'd want to garner national publicity, if you only have a local business. People aren't going to fly in from around the country to use your plumbing service, or buy insurance from you, or try the newest item on your menu, are they? Maybe, but probably not. So then, is national publicity a waste? Most people will probably tell you so. Most people will tell you to stay local, because that's where your bread and butter is.

Granted most people are going to want local media; that's where they live, that's where their business is based, that's where their money is going to come from, and that's where they're going to sell their products or services. So, why am I telling you to pitch the national press? Because, a national story will establish you as an expert in your field. You will be able to put your media credits in your releases and bios and, most importantly, national media can help drive your *local* media through the roof.

Let's say that you land a thirty-second quote on *CNN*. Now what? You move as quickly as possible and let your local media outlets know that you were recently featured on *CNN*. You, small-town businessperson from Nowhereville, USA, were featured on the national news. Heck, that in and of itself is news. Believe me, nothing impresses the media more than media. Now you're national news and you're in a position to garner local news. National media feeds the local media. It takes some thought, work, and persistence, but the rewards can be incredible.

If you initially don't land any national interest, don't let that deter or depress you. Keep at it, and remember, the process also works in reverse. Once you receive local publicity, you can use that as ammunition to approach the national media again. The local press is your main priority, that's where your emphasis should be. But don't overlook the national media. It can help establish you as an expert in your field and help you land major local stories.

I Don't Want To Be In The Media, I Just Want To Be Successful.

A lot of people have resistance to doing media. They don't want to do interviews, they don't want to be "stars," they just want their business to be successful. If you feel that way, ask yourself what you're willing to do to be successful. Are you willing to utilize the most powerful marketing tool available? Are you willing to utilize the magic of the media, and give your business a real chance for success?

An incredible new tool is being offered to those who are willing to utilize it. Effective media placement isn't about wanting to be a star or wanting to appear in the media—it's about success. It's about establishing yourself as an expert in your field and zooming beyond your competition. Publicity is a creative, effective, relatively inexpensive, and dynamic way to achieve success. You are not positioning yourself as a "star" or an entertainer, but as an expert in your field. You are establishing yourself as an invaluable resource for the media. You probably don't like to pay the bills, or do the books, or shop for your best suppliers, but you do it because it's part of doing business. It is a part of your bottom line. Media placement should also be an integral part of that equation. You do it because you want to be successful. Period.

I'm Not Interesting Enough To Do PR

Sure, the media interviewed you once, but that was just a fluke. You're too bland, too shy, your business is too dull, no one is going to care about anything you have to say. Why should you even bother trying publicity? It'll never work anyway.

I'm sure that there are some businesses that shouldn't utilize public relations. I suppose that if you're in the cloak-and-dagger field, you don't want to broadcast it all over the country. But this book is for the majority of people who can utilize the media to build their business, for entrepreneurs who want to start a new company or launch a new product, professionals who want to market their service, physicians who want to increase their practice, or artists who want to showcase their talents. Just about all of us fall into one of those categories. If you do, and you want to utilize the power of publicity, stop thinking negatively. Everyone is interesting, every business is interesting, every field has interesting stories to tell.

Remember, you are the only "you" around. No one does what you do quite like you do it. Whether you know it, or even want to believe it, you're an original, you're unique. So start viewing yourself that way.

Strange as it sounds, sometimes people who protest that they're boring or have nothing to say are some of the most egotistical folks around. You know the kind—they are setting the rest of us up to argue with them and convince them how fascinating and interesting they really are. Then there are those who, due to a real lack of self-esteem, honestly believe they're duller than dull and that no one on earth would want to hear about who they are or what they do.

If you belong to the first camp, stop playing that game, you're irritating everyone around you and in the long run, you're only hurting yourself. If you belong in the latter camp, you are mistaken —you are interesting. It's an issue you need to work on, whether you work on it in therapy or with friend. If you want to succeed, break through your negative self-image. It's important to start moving forward. Even if you don't believe that you're interesting or have an absorbing story to tell, start acting like you do. Take a deep breath, take some baby steps, and start pushing yourself out there. Action is remarkably powerful. If you take action, if you start treating yourself and presenting yourself as though you are worthy of success, success will start to come to you. You then start to see the truth and start to believe it. Don't wait until you *feel* important or successful.

Think of your business as a separate entity that deserves respect and caring. Start treating yourself and your business that way, and others will begin to react accordingly. In time, you'll start to internalize that sense of respect and success. You'll start to feel it yourself. I know it's hard, but don't let a poor self-image or lack of self-esteem keep you from achieving your dreams.

Sometimes it works to give yourself some distance from the situation. Stand outside of yourself. Hire yourself to represent your business. Become your business's publicity person. Try to view it objectively. How would you sell you if you weren't you, if you weren't stuck inside of you with all your doubts and your fears? How would you approach it? What would you do? What advice would you give? Be creative. Don't let your fears and doubts stop you. Remember, no matter how confident some people seem, everybody's afraid of not being interesting enough or not being success material. *We're all success material.* Part of achieving success is working through those doubts and fears.

I'll Grumble, Gripe And Complain

Your best quotes were cut from the story. You didn't like the way you looked. They forgot to mention where you're located. They gave the story a negative slant—and you're not going to stand for it! You're going to call that editor or segment producer and give him or her a piece of your mind. Wonderful. There's a word for what you're about to do—suicide. Never, ever, ever call and complain because you didn't like the way a story came out. If information, date, time, etc., was reported incorrectly, you can politely call to set the record straight, but if you weren't given the amount of time that you felt you warranted, if you weren't made the star, when you thought you were going to be the star, if other people were given more prominence than you, or even if you ended up being cut out of the article or segment altogether—those are the breaks. Use whatever coverage you received to get a better piece next time. You're going to run into these situations. I guarantee it. So come to terms with it now.

Realize that either you just didn't quite fit the piece (this happens sometimes) or your quotes didn't quite make it. Do some homework and give them a better interview next time. Make it a learning experience. But never, ever, call the media to complain that you weren't given enough space or enough time. There will be promises made that won't be kept. Stories will be killed (not used). Everything that you can imagine will happen. They're all learning experiences, and you go into the game knowing that.

The Grand Slam

One of the primary reasons people become so angry and bitter with publicity is because of what I call the grand slam mentality. Too many people believe that next TV interview or magazine article is going to be *it*. It's going to change their lives. That one story will turn it all around. All their problems will be over. Millions will pour in, they'll be able to move to the Bahamas and retire. Well, it doesn't happen that way. So you'd best come back to earth with the rest of us. You are doing publicity, not playing the lottery. I have had clients who have called, furious that their appearance on a national talk show or in a national magazine did not result in thousands of calls. One particular client was especially disappointed when her national TV spot only resulted in a couple of hundred calls in two days. Personally, I thought a couple of hundred calls from one segment was great. Even though those calls paid for my service many times over, they did not fulfill her grand slam expectations. It was not the super-jackpot, overnight, life-altering event she had hoped for.

Then again, rare as they are, grand slams do happen. Keep in mind, there is another side of the coin. Sometimes you'll hit a home run when you least expect it. Be prepared. There are times when what you think will be a small piece will turn into a major article or TV segment. So, even though you don't spend your time dreaming of hitting a grand slam, you had better prepare for hitting one.

Not long ago I worked with a small, struggling company that barely made enough to stay afloat. We were able to place what turned out to be a seven-minute segment on their product on a national TV program. The segment was perfect. We couldn't have done a better job of presenting the product in a positive light. Well, the piece struck a chord. It hit, and hit big. Calls poured in from all over the country. The demand was overwhelming, so much so that their phone lines blew. As far as we can figure, they received close to half a million calls in a little over a week. But they weren't prepared. The company that handled their telemarketing was not equipped to handle the amount of calls that came in. The company itself did not have enough product in stock to fulfill the demand. Furthermore, their supplier had a slow turn-around time, and, unbeknownst to me, they had not secured a merchant account and were unable to accept credit card orders over the phone. Eventually they were able to secure a merchant account and fulfill some of the orders. Here was an incredible media success story that was not utilized. They were not prepared to capitalize on what could have been a grand slam.

The moral is, you never know. So, do your best, get the interviews done, and then let 'em go. If it's not exactly what you wanted, there's always next time. Use that one quote, or that one sentence, or whatever you come away with, in your releases and bios. Use what you can and keep moving forward.

A Special Case—The Myth of the Artist

This myth is a bit different than the others, but it can be more devastating than all the others combined. This is a myth that can stop you from becoming successful, before you even start. I know from experience. I'm the best example of this myth in action, since I bought it, hook, line, and sinker.

From my first reading of *Catcher in the Rye* at the age of sixteen, I knew I wanted to be a writer, specifically a novelist. It was all I ever wanted, imagined, or fantasized about (girls aside). I shunned anything that had to do with business. Business was anathema. Salinger, Miller, and Kerouac were my role models. They never became businessmen and neither would I.

I left school to write. I wrote, published some poetry, and took odd jobs delivering newspapers and driving airport shuttles. Eventually, to help pay the rent, I began to work as a free-lance writer for a local music publication, which led to assignments with other publications. But this was no good. I was depressed by the fact that I was working as a music journalist; my calling was to write literature, not to interview rock stars. Still, I continued. I eventually began writing for national magazines and interviewing even more prominent rock stars. This had to stop as my entire artist-self was being compromised. So, I made a stand, albeit a subconscious one. One evening when I was scheduled to interview the Rolling Stones, I fell asleep. I missed the interview. But I was happy. I figured that my tainted life as a music journalist was over. Wrong. I continued to receive writing assignments in spite of my faux pas.

The worst part was that, although I was horrified by my fall from grace into the dark morass of journalism and shoddy commerce, a part of me was intrigued by publishing and marketing. I began to have daydreams about developing and launching my own magazines. How could I think such thoughts? Novelists led avant-garde lifestyles and wrote. There was no place for business or marketing in the writer's universe.

In my mind, real writers weren't business people, they were artists. But I never thought to question my definition of an artist. It took me quite a few years to realize that I fantasized more about the writer's lifestyle than the writer's work, and that fantasy in the end became a prison. Real writers write, that is their one directive. Whatever else they do, whatever lifestyle they lead, has nothing to do with the fact that they are writers. Moreover, I am amazed by the number of people who chose to live what they believe is the writer's lifestyle, in order to avoid the act of writing. Talk about marketing! That's the ultimate in image manipulation. That is the "if I appear to be a writer, painter, or musician, people will assume I am," school of art. What a sham. What a waste.

It took me several years to understand this most important fact of life: I am a writer, but I am also a businessman and an entrepreneur. But, the real surprise? I didn't have to make a choice between the businessman and the artist. There was no choice to make. They are both parts of who I am. I run a company and I write nonfiction books and novels.

So, if you find yourself trapped in the web of the artist's myth, save yourself some valuable time. Shatter the myth. Create your own myth. Become a great artist and a successful entrepreneur and business person. Those who insist that in order to be an artist you have to dress, live, think, and create in a prescribed way, are trapped in the myth themselves. They're not concerned with art, but with style and fashion. Forget about fashion. You are after substance. The bravest artists are trailblazers. They shatter the rules, destroy the stereotypes, and live life on their own terms. Forget about the artist's myth, or the business myth, or any other myth you might be trapped in. Trailblaze your own life. Create your own myth!

Chapter Thirteen

Great PR Mistakes

13

GREAT PR MISTAKES

Now that we've exploded the greatest publicity myths, let's move on to the most common and lethal publicity mistakes that you can make. These are the mistakes that I have run across most often. They can ruin a campaign. Do yourself a favor. Study them. Learn them. Avoid them.

The Renaissance Man Trap
aka
The Master of Everything

You may be very good at what you do. You may be well versed in a number of topics, but believe me, you don't know everything. None of us do. I don't know how many times I've heard a prospective client use the word genius to describe him or herself during an initial consultation. I am one who believes a healthy ego is a definite asset, but sometimes it's good to hold on to at least a minor dose of reality. When people assure me that they can discuss everything, I find they have real trouble focusing on anything. Generalists tend to remain just that, general. The media wants an expert. They want someone who is an authority, someone who is well versed on a certain topic or in a particular field.

One client gave me a list of topics he could address. The list included any and everything to do with health, as well as politics,

117

psychotherapy, metaphysics, entertainment . . . the list went on and on. I was tempted to ask him to give me a list of topics that he couldn't address. That would have saved me some time. The trouble was he actually thought that he could thoroughly address all of those topics, and, although I'm sure he could have discussed the various topics on the list, that's not the point. Anyone can discuss a topic. What the media wants is someone who is an expert, not someone who has opinions or is a great conversationalist.

But, let's suppose he had been an expert in all of those fields, it would still have been suicide to try and pitch him as Mr. Know-It-All. He would have lost all credibility. No one would have believed that he was an expert in everything. He would have been immediately dismissed. The campaign would have had no focus.

So, focus your message. What is your expertise? What can you talk about? Be specific. Focus your story. You may have numerous talents, you may have several stories to tell, but don't try to tell them all at once. You don't want a one-note campaign, but you do have to play each note individually. If you slam all the piano keys down at once, you get noise. What you're looking for is melody, music. You can tell your stories, just tell them one at a time.

Come up with five or six different topics or hooks that you can honestly address. Now put them in order. Prioritize them. Don't pitch them all at once. Keep your ego on a short leash. Not only can it lead you away from your goal and into a fantasy land, it can also alienate those around you, including the media. Be realistic. You're not doing this to satisfy your ego needs, but to build your business. Don't worry about not being able to discuss all the various topics that are near and dear to your heart. You'll get to them eventually. Right now you're developing hooks, story ideas. Eventually you can broaden your scope and move the focus to other topics. Be patient. Develop your stories, outline the particulars, be specific, and don't be a master of everything. Otherwise you'll be left alone up there in geniusland with no one to talk to.

I'm A Natural
aka
I Don't Need To Prepare For The Media

It's true that some people are better suited for interviews and for dealing with the media than others. There is such a thing as innate presence and star power. Some people just come off better than others. But, regardless of the field or endeavor, everyone needs to prepare and everyone improves with practice. The best way to approach a media campaign is to realize that, although you may be more prepared than others, you still have room to improve. You can gather more information. You can give a better, tighter interview. You can come up with newer, fresher story ideas. You can improve your sound bytes. You can refine your physical presentation. You constantly need to prepare and improve. You need to prepare your answers and anticipate the questions that are going to be asked. You have to prime yourself to handle a hostile or misinformed interviewer. You have to review your objectives and goals. Taking success for granted is one of the biggest and most foolish mistakes possible. Let your competition make those mistakes. Constantly reassess, refine, and reevaluate.

I Know What The Media Wants

The media wants stories, but beyond that, not even the media knows what it wants. The media is constantly searching, trying out new stories, coming up with new ideas. You have to study the various media outlets, review the different formats, study the types of stories they've run in the past. No one knows what the media wants because it's constantly changing. Don't take for granted you are some kind of media maven and that you know more than everyone else does. *Remember, you're going to succeed by learning how the media thinks, not by assuming you think they know what they want.* You have to prepare, do your homework, study the various media outlets. The bottom line is a good story, but don't assume because you find a story of interest, that the media will like it as well. Nine times out of ten, you're going to be wrong. Think like an editor, think like a producer. Once again, work backwards. Look at the particular media you are targeting. Who is the audience? What is the basic age range? Does it appeal to primarily men or women? What type of stories does it generally run? All right, now put yourself in the place of the editor or producer—how could you fit a story on your business, product, or talent into the format of that media outlet?

What story would work? What would the focus be?

For example, let's say that you are a fashion designer of men's clothing. *GQ* and *Esquire* would be natural media outlets to approach. You would need to come up with a hook that makes you and your designs special, but you know that with a little persistence and creativity you should be able to place a piece in those publications. What about *Vogue*? Why not? You could pitch a piece on yourself as the new up-and-coming designer who is reshaping the future of men's fashion, or a piece, aimed towards women, on How to Dress a Man for the Millennium. Let's say you wanted to go to *The Wall Street Journal*. Okay, pitch a story on dressing for success in the '90s, or an article on the business of fashion, or the inside workings of the fashion industry. Pitch the media according to its needs, not according to yours. Assume that the story you are dead set on telling isn't all that interesting to anyone besides yourself. Now, be creative, give it a spin. Give it a make-over. Make it newsworthy.

I Am Only Going To Talk About What I Want To Talk About

We all have different expressions, different moods, different topics we enjoy discussing. None of us have one-note personalities, but so many people try to launch one-note media campaigns. If you adamantly refuse to broaden the scope of your story, I hope your mother's a good listener, because there aren't a hell of a lot of other people whom you're going to reach. People who are inflexible, or have a one-note story, usually have failed media campaigns. Why? They're boring! When people think this way, it's generally because they erroneously believe that the rest of the world is just as fascinated by their ideas as they are. Well, they're wrong.

Most people are going to be bored to tears by what you think is the greatest thing ever. Now that doesn't mean that the topic is boring, but that your approach is. Remember, your job is to meet the media's needs. Broaden your scope. Come up with other ways to pitch your story. You'll be able to talk about your story, but not until you interest the media. And to do that, sometimes you have to use the indirect approach.

If you are a landscaper, you may want to pitch a story that has you critiquing the pros and cons of the White House grounds. That's not the story you probably particularly want to address. You want to tell people that you are a wonderful landscaper and that they should hire you, but there's no story there. By talking about the White House grounds, you have added another dimension. You have raised the stakes. You're not just discussing how to landscape Joe Blow's home, you're outlining how to best landscape the First Family's home. These are grounds that everyone has seen (at least in photos or TV) and can relate to. More importantly, you are establishing yourself as an expert in your field.

Be open to new ideas, brainstorm. Come up with as many ideas as you can. Let them be as crazy as you want—don't edit yourself. Now review your list and start to edit out the ideas that don't work. Formulate two or three new story angles. Write them up as releases. Broadening your scope will help ensure your success.

Forget Cable—I'm Only Doing The Majors

I've had clients tell me that they'd never even consider a community newspaper or cable access show. There was one prospective client who gave me a list of about ten media outlets. These were the only ones he was interested in and the only ones he'd appear in. They included *Oprah*, *Time*, *The Tonight Show*, and *USA Today*. Needless to say, we didn't work together, but this gives you some idea of how short-sighted people can be. Approach your media campaign this way, and you're dead in the water before you've even started. If you're not willing to be flexible or realistic, you're wasting your time and money. Media placement isn't about doing one or two big shows. It is

cumulative, it's a building process. Don't let your ego or preconceived ideas ruin your chances for success. *Media begets media*. A
cable show can lead to a community-based program, which can lead
to a feature on your local evening news. Appearing in a small magazine gives you powerful ammunition with which to approach a bigger
publication. Keep yourself on course. Even if you've done some larger press, don't discount the smaller media. Don't let your media
appearances go to your head. A dose of realism and humility will save
you a mountain of grief.

I'm Gonna Dazzle 'Em

It's press kit time again! You've got it, you're going to put together a
huge, glossy press kit, fill it with bios, press releases, fact sheets,
photos, graphs, statistics, brochures, covering everything that ever
happened in your life, with every possible bit of information that you
have on yourself and your company, and you're going to send it to every media outlet you can think of.

Interesting plan, if your aim is to throw money away and alienate
the media. To begin with, unless you have loads of disposable cash,
you're going to go broke. Also, it's going to be incredibly boring, not
to mention annoying for the media to receive all that information,
information they never requested. As I mentioned previously, press
kits can be effective, but only if they're used sparingly and shrewdly.
Don't inundate the media with information, and if you've hired a firm,
don't give them carte blanche in the matter. Too many PR firms have
a tendency to send out press kits en masse. It's a common practice,
but a wasteful one. Also, keep in mind, PR firms can make a heck of
a lot of money charging their clients for high-priced press kits.

Frills and fluff ain't gonna cut it. Buy yourself some two-pocket
folders at any stationery store. Buy a good medium-priced folder; you
don't want the most expensive, but you don't want the cheapest folder
either. Inside the folder include copies of any articles or interviews
you have appeared in, a fact sheet, a short bio about you and your
company, a press release, and any visuals or photos that you believe

are important. No fluff, only include the pertinent stuff. That is your press kit. First send a release, make a follow-up call. If a producer or editor asks for a kit, send one, but only to people who have requested it. Be selective. Be smart.

Also, consider changing your press kit to fit the media that you're sending to. You may not want to send the same press kit to *Time* magazine that you would to *Runner's World* or *Forbes*. Be discerning in who you send the kits to and in the materials you include. Also be sure to modify your press kit to fit the needs of the media that you're sending it to.

Either They Interview Me Monday At Noon Or It's Off

I know, you have a busy schedule, you have a job to do, a business to run, products to sell. Your time is valuable. Who does the media think they are? They think that you can just drop whatever you're doing to do an interview when they want to do it? It's inconvenient. It's not fair. But it's reality. Although you will usually have time to plan and arrange your schedule, there are going to be times that the media wants to do an interview and wants to do it immediately, or wants to schedule it at a time that is inconvenient, or reschedules it at the last minute, forcing you to, once again, change your plans.

Those are the breaks. There are going to be times when you're just not going to be able to accommodate the media's schedule. There are going to be some interviews that you'll have to miss. But only miss an interview if it's completely unavoidable—the plague, an alien invasion—you get the picture. You may be annoyed, and you may be angry, but if you can possibly arrange your schedule so that you can make the interview, do it. The press isn't purposely trying to inconvenience you. You wouldn't believe the amount of times that an editor or producer has to switch from one story to another on a moment's notice. A million things can come up. A fire, an international breaking story, a Presidential speech, any number of stories are going to preempt you. This is just the nature of the business. It happens all the time.

It does you no good to take your anger out on the interviewer or the producer. It was not done to harm you. The decision was circumstantial. Always keep your objective in mind. Your objective is to build your business, to create success. And you're going to accomplish your goal by reaching as many people as you can. Your objective is to do those interviews, not to alienate the press. Remember, press begets press. Every interview you do is helping to pave your way to greater success.

If You Don't Run This Story, I'm Taking It To Your Competition

How many people do you know who react well to threats or ultimatums? You are trying to position yourself as a media resource or an ally, and an ally does not issue threats. You want the media to understand that you can help meet their needs by giving them interesting stories. You are not going to make your story more interesting to a newspaper editor or TV producer by threatening to take your story to his or her competitor.

If your story is hot or timely, and various media outlets are pursuing you, by all means, use that interest to your advantage. Inform the media outlets that there are others interested and that you need to make a decision as soon as possible. Try to negotiate the best coverage you can. But, even in that situation, *you never want to threaten the media.*

If you can convince the media that you have an interesting story that meets their needs and that you are an expert in the field, the media will feature you. Those are your primary objectives. You can threaten, scream, cry, and badger the media, but all you are going to do is alienate them. Plenty of people do these things every day. Of course, you'll never see them in the media.

Because we humans are so creative, and come up with an infinite variety of ways to err, this is by no means an all-inclusive list of mistakes. But, these are the most common ones. Engrave them into your brain, and never, ever make them.

Chapter Fourteen

Not Even One Phone Call?

14

NOT EVEN ONE PHONE CALL?

A magazine ran a story on you. You were confident that this article was going to be a big one, and you were prepared. You went so far as to add additional phone lines to handle the hundreds, maybe even thousands, of calls that you knew would be jamming your lines. So, the story came out and—nothing. Not a single call. As far as you know, not a living soul saw it. You are crushed. "That's it!" you yell, pounding your fist on the desk. "No more PR!" You've been spinning your wheels, wasting time and money, and for what? For nothing! You've had it. No more publicity. PR doesn't work and you are a prime example that it doesn't work. You are the consummate illustration of a media failure story. Right?

Wrong. But, understandably, trying to explain that the preceding scenario is not the story of a media failure to clients who have had similar experiences is perhaps the hardest part of my job. If I were handling your campaign, I too would be disappointed that the article did not elicit a response, but in the overall scheme of things, I'd think that article was a great tool for us to use in the future. To be effective in this field you have to look at the big picture. Your short-term goals were not met by the particular article in question, but it affords you new, powerful ammunition to reach your long-term goals. It helps establish you as an expert in your field and separates you from your competition. It gives you yet another media tear sheet that you can use in your press kit, another article that you can pull quotes from for your press releases and bios.

But if nobody saw it, what good can it do you? Plenty. To begin with, you don't know who saw it. You never know. In five days, three weeks, or six months, you may start receiving calls. Sometimes people don't need your product or service at the time they see your story, but they write down your number to contact you at a later date. I've seen this happen over and over again.

Working Your Media

But let's say you never receive one call as a result of that article. It's still valuable. You just need to work it. Become the story's distributor—and I mean distributor in the most basic sense—circulate your story, spread the word, mention the story in your biography and fact sheet, use it when pitching other stories, let other media outlets know that you were featured in the article. Duplicate it and use it as a press sample. Use quotes from the story in your mailers, newsletters, ads, and marketing to help cement your existing client base. If you have employees, distribute it through your company as a form of internal publicity. If used correctly, you can turn this article into a powerful marketing tool.

I understand being temporarily depressed if you don't get a decent response to a story, which is why it is so important to understand exactly how media placement works. By understanding the process, you turn what appears to be a lost opportunity into a tremendous advantage. Be creative. Make a list of the various ways you can utilize your media, from ads and newsletters to placing framed copies of articles in your window or office. Don't let your failed expectations cloud your business sense. Don't waste opportunities due to short sightedness. Be imaginative, inventive. Think.

Even When It Works, There's More Work

Now let's suppose that article has the exact effect that you're hoping for. The phones are ringing day and night. Both your business and your bank account are flourishing. Success! Now you can forget about that story and move on. No. No. No. Whether the article elicits a negligible response or a huge response, you still need to work it. This is where most people fail to understand the process. Because their short-term goals were met, they stop in mid-process and neglect their long-term goals.

We were once retained by a young actress who perfectly illustrated this point. She had been a regular in a prime time TV series. The series had been canceled, and she wanted to do more work in the feature film industry. During the time that the series was on TV, she had received a mountain of press, including stories in *People*, and *The Los Angeles Times*, as well as on *Entertainment Tonight*, but when I asked to see copies or video of some of her media, she just stared at me. She hadn't kept any. While she had been on the series, the media exposure had accomplished its short-term work, keeping her in the public eye, and that's all she had been concerned with. She never looked at her long-term goals. The media coverage she had received was worth its weight in gold, but she didn't see it. Learn from her mistake. In this business you not only need to see the forest, but the trees, grass, and bushes, as well as all the furry animals along the way.

You're Placing A Story Where?

Every client's happy when we place them on *Today* or in *Newsweek*, but they're not quite as overjoyed when we place them on a relatively insignificant cable show or in an obscure magazine they've never heard of. I know there are times my clients find my choice of media placements bewildering. The media outlets are too small, too insignificant, too obscure. They don't reach the client's direct-target market. Why do it—there will be no response. It's a waste of time and money.

By now, you have probably anticipated my response. We place the stories, because we know that we can use them to our advantage. It's important to have a broad perspective and see the whole picture. The process isn't as obvious as it may seem at first glance. Instead of just asking if a particular story will bring in immediate clients or calls, ask yourself if that story will help you garner other media, or will it be useful to you in your overall marketing plan.

That's What Makes It Magic

What truly makes this process magical is that when you appear in the media, regardless of how big or how small the outlet, you never know who's going to see it or what opportunity is going to come your way. A local Los Angeles-based newspaper once ran a story on my company, which elicited almost no response. I was a bit disappointed, but it was a great article and made for a wonderful tear sheet to use in my media package. A few weeks later I received a call from an author in Florida who had been sent a copy of the article and wanted to hire us. Florida? In three weeks I had not received one call from the Los Angeles area in response to the article, and here I was receiving a call from Florida. Apparently a friend of the author, who lives in Southern California, had seen the piece and mailed it to her. The author explained that the article, which focused on my firm's ability to place clients on national talk shows, interested her. Her book was about to be published, and she wanted to appear in the national media, especially talk shows. She signed with us, and we were able to launch a very successful campaign for her. Our relationship with the author resulted in our working with other writers. So, even though the article only brought us one phone call, that one call was a great one.

I've had clients refuse to appear on cable shows because they believed cable was not prestigious enough, but I've also worked with clients who have received huge benefits from appearing on local cable shows. You just never know, and if you don't do the interviews and utilize your press, you never will.

When you start a publicity campaign you have a set of objectives in mind that you are hoping to accomplish, but, as I said before, what makes media placement such a fascinating field is that you never know who you are going to reach. Because you have the ability to reach millions of people, you will be continually surprised by the results of a campaign. Some of the most interesting results that have come from our media placement are ones that neither I nor my clients would have ever imagined. I have had clients offered their own TV pilots and approached to become partners in new business ventures. In one instance, a financier, who happened to catch a TV segment that one of our clients was on, contacted the client and eventually bankrolled an entire new business for him. All of these opportunities came about because of exposure and visibility. Media is remarkably powerful. In one way or another, media touches all of our lives, influencing our thoughts, our beliefs, and our decisions. It is a forceful tool, and it can have amazing results.

Because of the unique power of the media, my clients have been afforded the opportunity to personally visit millions of homes, offices, airports, and restaurants, all within a single day. That is why it's magic.

Chapter Fifteen

Utilizing Your Press

15

UTILIZING YOUR PRESS

Throughout this book, I've mentioned various ways that your press and media can be utilized. It's a part of the publicity process that I can't emphasize enough. This is an area where most people stumble. Too many people only look for the immediate results that a magazine article, radio interview, or TV segment can bring. In this simplistic equation, if a story brings in clients, patients, or, at the very least, inquiries from prospective clients, it was a success, and, if it did not, it was a failure. There are countless ways in which you can effectively utilize copies of articles or tapes of programs you have appeared in. This media exposure can be like gold if utilized properly. But this is where you really have to do both work and homework. This is the one area where, even if you have hired a PR firm, you're on you own.

Most PR firms will place you in the media and use your media appearances to interest other media outlets in interviewing you. But don't rely on a public relations firm to fully maximize the various ways that your media can help your business or career grow. That's not their job. Their objective is to secure you media and to implement a successful campaign. Your job is to be inventive and creative and to effectively utilize your media in as many ways as possible. How? The following is a list of various ways to effectively utilize your media; study it, add to it, and come up with your own ideas.

Utilizing Your Media

1. **Media Begets Media**

Use your TV and radio appearances and magazine and newspaper articles to interest other media. Remember, media begets media. Copy the article, video, or audio tape and send it out when the media requests further information on you. Update your biography to include your most recent media appearances. When writing or talking to the media, let them know about other segments or articles you have appeared in. Be prudent in the media you send. If a feature story or interview has certain quotes you are unhappy with, you may want to copy only the parts of the interview you want highlighted. If you have a recently taped interview from a particular TV program and are now being considered by their direct competitor, you may want to think twice before sending that particular tape for viewing.

2. **Display, Display**

Keep copies of articles displayed in your office or framed on your walls. Don't hide your media. Also consider making copies of TV or radio interviews to show to your clients, customers or patients, as well as to your prospective clients and customers. Display your press. You will be perceived differently. Showing your media also helps to stimulate word of mouth. People love to tell their friends that they are seeing or working with a "celebrity."

3. **Use The Magic In Your Marketing**

Mention your media in your ads, flyers, newsletters, and brochures. Review your articles and interviews, and look for any particularly impressive quotes about you or your business that you can highlight in your ads or marketing.

If you have a staff or employees, teach them to use the media you have been featured in in their pitches or conversations to both clients and prospective clients. Teach your employees to utilize your media.

If they are talking to a prospective client, patient, or customer, it never hurts to have them mention that you, your product, or service were featured in a magazine or TV program. Work with them, come up with ways to weave your media appearances into their conversations and discussions.

4. **Make Sure They See You**

Send out copies of your media tear sheets to your current and prospective clients. If possible, send them along with a short note, stating that you thought they'd enjoy reading the piece. Also, mail out notices alerting your clients, customers, or prospects whenever an article or interview is going to run. A word of caution here: announcing that you're going to be featured in an upcoming TV segment on a particular day and time can sometimes be tricky. I can't tell you how many times we have had a show's air date changed on us at the last minute.

5. **Using Your News To Network**

If you give seminars, speeches, or lectures, use copies of your print tear sheets and videotaped interviews in your presentations. It will help pique the audience's interest and instantly establish you as an expert in your field. Always use your media exposure to network with other professionals in your field. Once you're viewed as an expert, new alliances and working relationships tend to occur.

Consider hiring a graphic artist to help professionally display your articles and interviews. Make your press work as hard as you do. These are just some examples of ways to utilize your press. With a little thought and ingenuity, you'll come up with several more.

Chapter Sixteen

Author, Author—
*   I've Published a Book*
*   .....Now What?*

16

AUTHOR, AUTHOR—
I'VE PUBLISHED A BOOK—
NOW WHAT?

So you finally did it. You wrote that book you've been threatening to write, sent it to publishers, amassed a mountain of rejection slips, but finally found the right publisher. Your manuscript was accepted. You're going to be a published author. Great—you can now turn your attention to your next book. Your first book's finished; your publisher will take care of everything from here on in. Surprise!

At my firm, we run the gamut when it comes to representing authors, from self-published, first-time writers, to writers who have landed multi-book deals with major publishers and, I am sad to report, the one common link among all the authors we work with is that, unless their names happen to be Anne Rice, Stephen King, or Tom Clancy, none seem to receive much publicity support.

It would be easy to blame the publishing company's publicity departments, but that's not the problem. Most publishing companies have slashed their in-house publicity staffs and the publicists are overloaded. Every month, up to thirty books are dumped on one or two in-house publicists. It's an impossible task. What has happened is that many in-house publicity departments have been reduced to little more than direct marketing departments. They send out books, press kits and press releases and hope for the best. They have neither the time nor the manpower to make follow-up calls. And unless you have name recognition or have written a shocking exposé that the entire world is waiting to read, chances are you and your book will get lost in the shuffle.

Whether you are self-publishing or are publishing your book through a major house, this is one instance where I strongly recommend you hire a firm that understands book publicity to implement your campaign. Books are time-sensitive. This is one time you don't have the luxury of learning as you go. Although you hope that your book will become a classic and continue to sell throughout the years, your book has a shelf life. You need to launch an effective publicity campaign even before it's published. If you want to have it reviewed, you need to send a copy of your book, or the galleys, to reviewers, often as long as three months before the publication date. Once it's published, you immediately want to hit the local media, the talk shows, and the national press. One area you definitely want to focus on is national and regional radio. There are hundreds of regional and local radio talk shows and current event-oriented programs that feature books and authors. These interviews are almost always conducted over the phone. You can be at home in your bathrobe, discussing your book, while thousands of people listen.

If you are publishing with a major house, I suggest that you approach the matter as though you're self-publishing your book. View your publisher primarily as a distributor and assume that all of the responsibility for securing publicity for your book rests firmly on your weary shoulders. If your publisher actually launches a campaign for you, that's great, but don't count on it. You don't have the luxury of being wrong. If you assume the publicity will be done for you and it's not, by the time you discover your error, it will be too late. You will have missed your window of opportunity.

Pitch The Story, Not Your Book

If, due to lack of funds or other reasons, you choose to launch your own book publicity campaign, use the steps I've outlined in this book. Remember it still all comes back to the media hook. It's the story that will interest the press. Don't simply send out your book and information to the media, thinking that they'll be so knocked out by your writing or the book's subject matter that they'll be clamoring to interview you. It seldom works that way. Continue to develop hooks and story ideas that you can use to spotlight your book. If your book is non-fiction or how-to this becomes a much easier task. We have represented authors who have written books on fashion, beauty, health, relationships, sex, and a variety of other topics. Even though we focus on the books in our campaigns, we do not limit ourselves to the book exclusively. Our objective remains the same: to establish our clients as experts in their field. The book becomes a part of the story, but it never overwhelms the entire campaign. If you can place an article in a magazine or a segment on a talk show that revolves specifically around your book, you've hit pay dirt. But that's not an easy task. Certainly pitch your book as one of your hooks, but don't limit your campaign. Come up with other story ideas which can include your book, but do not revolve specifically around it.

For example, we worked with a psychotherapist who wrote a book on how to save a troubled marriage. Although we included the book in all of our pitches, the focus remained on the psychotherapist's expertise in relationship issues. We pitched the women's magazines and talk shows, relationship-oriented stories in which our client could appear as an expert. The media reacted well to our pitches and interviews were scheduled. Although some of the stories were about marriages and romantic relationships, others were about parent-child or sibling relationships. Even though those issues did not revolve specifically around the topic of our client's book, she could expertly address them. When she appeared on talk shows, our client was introduced as the author of her book and was asked questions about her book during the interview. Although the shows themselves did not always revolve around the book, the book and client were always highlighted.

If you have written a novel, your task is more difficult, but not impossible. Review all of your potential story ideas. Is there a reason you wrote the novel that could be turned into a pitch? Does your novel have to do with a specific field or realm that could be fashioned into a pitch? Is there something about you, your life or background that is newsworthy? Does your novel reflect any social trends or news stories that you can focus on? You were creative enough to write the novel, call upon that creativity once again. Make a list of all the potential story ideas and start writing again—writing press releases, that is.

But My Book's Self-Published

You'll be happy to know that, when it comes to media placement, it just doesn't matter anymore whether your book is published by a major house or is self-published. During all the time I've been representing authors, only once did I come across an objection to running a story because an author's book was self-published. We had placed an author, who had written a book on nutrition, on *CNN*. A day before the interview was scheduled, we received a call from the producer saying that they had decided to scrap the piece. When asked why, it turned out that the producer's superiors had balked because our client's book was self-published. We explained that the author and his book had been featured in both *Newsweek* and *USA Today*, but it seemed to make no impact on the producer. Three hours later we received another call stating that they had thought it over and decided that it didn't matter if the book was self-published or not. The interview went on as scheduled. The moral is, don't worry. A self-published author's real struggle has to do with distribution and marketing. When it comes to publicity, if you do it right, you can play in the same ballpark as the majors. As a matter of fact, I sometimes think that self-published writers fare better than their house-published counterparts because they are under no illusions. They don't assume that some big entertainment conglomerate is going to use all of its muscle and turn their book into an overnight sensation. They realize that if success is going to happen, they'd better get to work, and fast.

Writing and publishing a book is like giving birth. It ain't easy. The last thing you want to do is go through the process and not give your offspring a fighting chance. Your book was written to be read. Use the magic of the media. Get it out there.